Purchased book
11-1-82

Catch the
Little Foxes
That Spoil
the Vine

Catch the Little Foxes That Spoil the Vine

William E. Thorn

Fleming H. Revell Company
Old Tappan, New Jersey

Unless otherwise identified, Scripture quotations are from the King James Version of the Bible.

Scripture quotations identified RSV are from the Revised Standard Version of the Bible, copyrighted 1946, 1952, © 1971 and 1973.

Library of Congress Cataloging in Publication Data

Thorn, William E
   Catch the little foxes that spoil the vine.

   1.   Christian life—Baptist authors.   I.   Title.
BV4501.2.T514   248'.48'61   79-21749
ISBN 0-8007-1096-7

TO *the Dallas Baptist College family*
    for their
      encouragement,
        patience,
          understanding,
            through the years.
    I shall be eternally grateful.

Contents

Preface

In presenting these essays, I am aware of my limitations in the literary field! These little moral themes, delivered to local civic and school groups, were adapted to the particular time, place, and occasion. Part of the charm of these stories lies in extemporaneous delivery: The method of telling gives them their force.

A note of appreciation is extended to many friends who have encouraged me in this effort. Special appreciation is expressed to Mrs. Richard Garner, who has given of her time unselfishly to type and correct the manuscript. Without her able assistance, *Catch the Little Foxes That Spoil the Vine* could not have been completed.

W. E. THORN

Foreword

It was Socrates who taught in Athens some twenty-three centuries ago and who wrote these words of wisdom: "The power to speak well is taken as the surest index of a sound understanding; and discourse which is true and lawful and just is the outward image of a good and faithful soul."

These comments from the ancient teacher describe the content and the author of this volume. Dr. William E. Thorn is a master preacher, storyteller, and after-dinner speaker. His genius as a pulpiteer he received as a gift from his heavenly Father, and as an inheritance from his earthly father—Dr. F. B. Thorn—who was one of the great Gospel preachers of the George W. Truett, I. E. Gates, and L. R. Scarborough era.

As one reads these pages, one becomes conscious of being in the presence of a great artist at work, creating word pictures that strike the chords of the heart, soul, and mind.

To get the most from these messages, one must bring to them an imagination that understands the facts, a faith that interprets the facts, and a sense of humor that appreciates the way the facts are presented. These great themes reveal Dr. Thorn at his best. They sing of earthly and heavenly things. Underneath the quick-moving and entertaining content is a deep and genuine understand-

11

ing of the true nature of things—a theology true to divine revelation, reason and common sense, and personal experience.

If your religion is such that it hurts you to laugh and cry, don't read this book! But, if you need a lift and real blessing, read it and pass it on to a friend.

FRED A. WHITE
Vice-President for Academic Affairs
Dallas Baptist College

Catch the Little Foxes That Spoil the Vine

1

Little Threads That Bind Big Men

For precept must be upon precept, precept upon precept; line upon line, line upon line; here a little, and there a little.

Isaiah 28:10

Jonathan Swift was an English clergyman, poet, political writer, and satirist who was born in Dublin, Ireland, in 1667. His bid to worldly acclaim came in 1726 when he published his famous *Travels of Lemuel Gulliver*. It immediately became popular and ever since has captured the imagination of young and old alike. It has the reputation of being the best-known satire in the English language. In Swift's famous letter to Alexander Pope in 1725, he said, "I like the scheme of our meeting after distresses and dispersions, but the chief aim I propose to myself in all my labor is, to vex the world rather than divert it. . . . I have every hatred for all nations, pro-

15

fessions, and communities, and all my love to individuals."

Swift succeeded in vexing only a very few individuals. On the contrary, he diverted the world exceedingly for the simple reason that individuals laughed at his wit and presumably felt themselves to be excluded from his general satire.

The story of Gulliver concerns itself with voyages to very strange lands; it is divided into four books. The first is by far the most popular. Lemuel Gulliver travels first to the land of Lilliput, the land of Pygmies. The little people have a highly organized civilization. Swift makes the Lilliputians the means of satire by presenting these small creatures as possessed of the same political systems, motives, and vanities as mortal men. He causes readers to laugh at their antics for much the same reason that grownups are apt to laugh at the imitative ways of children.

As the story continues, Gulliver is washed ashore in the land of Lilliput. As he sleeps on the shore, he is discovered by these strange little people. They are just one-twelfth the size of normal men. As he sleeps, they tie him down with little threads. Each thread is a trifle and can easily be broken. The little people use hundreds of these threads, until it is impossible for Gulliver to break loose. He is now the prisoner of these little people.

Gulliver was not the first nor the last big man to be captured by little threads. Being little, they seem insignificant, and many a man discovers too late that the littleness of little things is bigger than he thought. Before we know it, we are victims.

A farmer's boy decided to get married. His father said to him, "John, when you get married, your liberty is gone."

The boy said he did not believe it. The father said, "I'll prove it to you. Catch a dozen chickens, tie their legs together and put them in the wagon. Hitch up the two horses to the wagon and drive into town. Stop at every house you come to, and wherever you find the man is boss, give him a horse. Wherever you find the woman is boss, give her a chicken. You'll give away all your chickens and come back with two horses."

The boy accepted the proposition and drove to town. He had stopped at every house and had given away ten chickens when he came to a nice little house and saw an old man and his wife standing out on the front lawn. He called to them and asked, "Who is boss here?"

The man said, "I am."

Turning to the woman, the boy said, "Is he boss?"

The woman replied, "Yes, he's boss."

The boy asked them to come down to the street. He then explained his reason for asking and told the man to pick out one of the horses. He said he would bring the horse back to him that afternoon. The old man and the old lady looked over the horses carefully, and the husband said, "I think the black horse is the better of the two."

The wife then said, "I think that bay horse is in every way the better horse. I would choose him."

The old man took a careful look at the bay horse and said, "I guess I'll take the bay horse."

The boy smiled and said, "No, you won't; you'll take a chicken."

The problem makes me think about a bit of folk poetry from the Song of Solomon: "Catch us the foxes, the little foxes, that spoil the vineyards . . ." (2:15 RSV). No one knows who wrote the words or what they meant to the person who wrote them, but they have fascinating possibilities.

How many little foxes there are that spoil the vineyard! It is also true with the little threads. Strong, heavy ropes aren't needed. Neither are huge beasts, such as lions or bears. Cataclysmic "acts of God," such as whirlwinds or earthquakes aren't necessary—just many little threads. They often look harmless but work havoc with big men. These little threads are dangerous. Little weaknesses become big ones. We meet great faults head-on; little ones are slippery.

We could suggest many of these little threads. There is the little thread of gossip, cheap reading, profanity, gambling, social drinking, lying, cheating, or even prejudice.

Today it would be well for us to consider some of these little threads that bind big men.

The Little Thread of Jealousy

Anyone who doubts jealousy's existence has only to recall some of the secrets of his own heart.

Dr. Roy Pearson, the noted clergyman and author, says that jealousy is a form of amnesia; the sufferer has forgotten who he is. A jealous man has no smoothness to his contours. His personality is bounded by sharp edges, and by being "edgy," he inspires edginess in those around him. His being suspicious of everyone, makes everyone suspicious of him.

Jealousy and envy are as old as the human race. The trail of sorrow began just outside Eden and reaches to the present moment. Cain slew his brother, Abel, in a jealous rage. Paul includes envy in his catalog of sins in Galatians 5:19–21, and James points out, "For where envying and strife is, there is confusion and every evil work" (James 3:16).

We criticize our competitors. We become angry and vindictive toward those who interfere with our status and prestige. How easy it is for the ugly girl to criticize the pretty girl's morals and manners. How much simpler to condemn our superiors than to improve ourselves. We become so self-important.

A Texas businessman rushed up to the ticket counter at the airport terminal and said hurriedly, "Give me a ticket on the next plane!"

"Where to, sir?" asked the ticket agent.

"Anywhere, son," said the Texan. "I've got business all over."

Even preachers become jealous of one another. A minister once complained to a friend that Billy Sunday had preached one of his sermons.

"How many people did Mr. Sunday convert with your sermon?" asked the friend.

"Three hundred," was the answer.

"How many did you convert with it?" continued the friend.

"None," said the minister.

"Then," said the friend, "let Billy Sunday have your sermon; he can do more with it than you can." For the same reason we should let God have our lives.

Pangs of jealousy were in Miss Iceberg's heart when she heard that her former admirer had proposed to Miss Lovewell. She happened to run across her in a bargain-basement rush. She could not resist giving a dig. "I hear that you've accepted Jack's proposal," she gushed. "I suppose he never told you he once proposed to me."

"No," answered Jack's fiancée. "He once told me there were a lot of things in his life of which he was ashamed, but I didn't ask him what they were."

Jealousy is the destroyer of beauty. People are inclined to exaggerate the faults of others and gossip about them. Perhaps this is natural, but it is foolish. The cavity in my tooth feels larger when I put the end of my tongue in it. This is because of the natural inclination of the tongue to exaggerate. I have not been inclined to criticize my friends, neither have I paid too much attention to my critics. I have never heard of a statue being erected in memory of a critic.

Many big men have missed their opportunities because of this little, ugly sin. They could never find greatness in themselves because their time was spent in seeking the ugliness in others.

Beware of this little thread of jealousy.

The Little Thread of Discouragement

In the garden of every life the ugly dragon of discouragement lifts its head. Many flee, some give up, but others face it with confidence and faith.

Saint Francis of Assisi, hoeing his garden, was asked what he would do if he were to learn that he was to die at sunset that very day. He replied, "I would finish hoeing my garden."

This little thread is usually found in most men. So many are discouraged about the uncertainty of the future. Discouragement can become an attitude. It is a habit for many. Recently a friend handed me this little statement about being gloomy.

Get a Transfer

If you are on the Gloomy Line, get a transfer. If you're inclined to fret and pine, get a transfer. Get off the track of Doubt and Gloom; get on the Sunshine Train—there's room—get a transfer.

If you are on the Worry Train, get a transfer. You must not stay there and complain—get a transfer. The Cheerful cars are passing through, and there is lots of room for you—get a transfer.

If you are on the Grouchy Train, get a transfer. Just take a Happy Special back—get a transfer. Jump on the train and pull the rope that lands you at the state of Hope—get a transfer.

AUTHOR UNKNOWN

Trouble, it seems, defies the law of gravity. It's easier to pick up than to drop.

A circus had a lion and a lamb in the same cage. A man looking at them asked the attendant if they got along together all right. The attendant replied, "Most of the time; now and then we have to put in a new lamb."

Someone said, "You are as young as your hope and as old as your despair." Discouragement is a sign of the lack of faith in oneself and God.

The pretty girl of the party was bantering with the genial bachelor about his reasons for remaining single.

"No, I never was exactly disappointed in love," he mused. "I was more what you might call discouraged. You see when I was very young, I became very much enamored with a young lady. I was mortally afraid to tell her of my feelings, but at last I worked up the courage to the proposing point and said, 'Let's get married.' "

" 'Goodness!' she exclaimed in reply. 'Who'd have us?' "

Others are discouraged by words they hear. Some things are merely make-believe.

Two prominent physicians, who had been called in consultation, retired to another room to discuss the sick one's condition. In the closet of that room was a small boy who had been told by the patient to hide in order to listen.

"Well, Jimmy," asked the patient eagerly after the physicians had gone. "What did they say?"

"I couldn't tell you that," said the boy, "because they used such big words that I couldn't understand 'em. All that I remember is that one of the doctors said to the other, 'Well, we'll soon find out at the autopsy.' "

In the congregation of a small-town church was a young bride whose husband was an usher. During the Sunday-morning service, she became terribly worried that she may have left the roast cooking in the oven. She wrote a note to her husband and passed it to him by way of another usher. The latter, thinking it was a note for the pastor, hurried down the aisle and laid it on the pulpit. Stopping abruptly in the middle of his sermon to read the note, the astonished pastor was met with the written injunction: "Please go home and turn off the gas."

The spirit of man should never cease to grow. Peter said, ". . . add to your faith virtue; and to virtue knowledge; And to knowledge temperance; and to temperance patience; and to patience godliness; And to godliness brotherly kindness; and to brotherly kindness charity" (2 Peter 1:5–7).

These are some qualities in which one can always continue to grow and become more beautiful in character.

This little thread of discouragement can become as strong as chains of iron.

Paul Dietzel tells that while football coach of Army, he was so downcast when Army lost to Navy that he wanted to call his wife and get a few words of love and affection to massage his ego. Not having any change, he turned to an army cadet and said, "Lend me a dime to call a friend." The cadet gave him twenty cents and said, "Call *all* of your friends."

Beware of the little thread of discouragement.

Men of faith—arise. Whether it be Abraham's going out not knowing whither, or Moses' leading the children of Israel, or Lincoln's guiding a nation in the crisis of its history, or Billy Graham's preaching the Gospel, we need men of faith.

Every man who is opening up new fields and enterprises or doing something unusual is a new proof to us that men do believe and that they receive according to their faith.

I am reminded of the wonderful story given to the world by John Bunyan. In his immortal story of man's journey from this world to that which is to come, Bunyan brings Christian and Hopeful to the "River of Death." There stood before them two men dressed in raiment that shone like gold, who informed them of the River of Death. The men said, "You will find it deeper or shallower as you believe in the King."

So it is in life. It depends on our faith in the King.

Beware of the little thread of discouragement.

The Little Thread of Laziness

Another little thread is the thread of laziness. An old German proverb states: "A young idler, an old beggar." Idleness is the refuge of weak minds and the holiday of fools. The idle brain is the devil's workshop. While the devil tempts all other men, idle men tempt the devil.

An idle man said he could not find bread for his family.

"Neither can I," said an industrious man standing near. "I have to work for all the bread I get."

Two deaf mutes, a man and his wife, were on the front porch of their home making signs at each other. The lady was working two of her fingers like a pair of scissors. The man was moving his arms as though he were swimming. Two men on the sidewalk became interested in the actions of the mute couple, and one asked the other, who knew something about the sign language, what they were saying.

The friend replied, "She is telling him to go cut the lawn; he's telling her to jump in the river."

Recently I found *Lincoln's Ten Guidelines* to accomplishment. Most lazy men disbelieve these excellent points:

Lincoln's Ten Guidelines

You cannot bring about prosperity by discouraging thrift.

You cannot help small men by tearing down big men.

You cannot strengthen the weak by weakening the strong.

You cannot lift the wage earner by pulling down the wage payer.

You cannot help the poor by destroying the rich.

You cannot keep out of trouble by spending more than your income.

You cannot further brotherhood of man by inciting class hatred.

You cannot establish security on borrowed money.

You cannot build character and courage by taking away man's initiative and independence.

You cannot help men permanently by doing for them what they could and should do for themselves.

Around the beginning of the sixteenth century, among the artists working in Rome, there was a universal complaint. All the good subjects for great art, they said, had already been used and unless a man were able to travel to obscure and exotic places, he could find nothing worthy of his talents. To the lazy artists, this was an excuse for idleness; to the incompetent, an excuse for mediocre work.

There was one man, the great Raphael, however, who did not believe this. He knew there were subjects everywhere in Rome, if the artists could only see them. Perhaps this is why he chose to saunter through the alleys and side streets rather than along the boulevards. On such a walk one day, he espied a woman seated in a tumbledown doorway holding a child to her breast. This was a commonplace scene, but there was something that was not commonplace about this particular woman. Raphael, the artist, saw it in an instant. He did not have paints or canvas, only a sketching pencil. He did not want to come back later and ask this woman to model the scene for him; he wanted her just as she was.

Fortunately, an unknown merchant had discarded a barrel head in the alley. It was clean enough for his purpose. Quickly he sketched the woman and the child. Back in his studio, Raphael converted his rough sketch into the beautiful *Madonna of the Chair*.

This painting may not be among his best-known works, but many of the unremembered artists who could find no subjects worthy of their talents would have liked to have had the honor of painting it.

Thomas Edison was showing a party of friends his beautiful summer residence. It was equipped with many labor-saving devices. One exception, however, was a turnstile so stiff that it required considerable strength to force a passage.

One by one the guests pushed through. At last, one of them ventured to say, "Mr. Edison, why do you have everything so perfect except this awful turnstile?"

"Ah," replied the host, his eyes twinkling, "everybody who pushed the turnstile pumped eight gallons of water into the tank on my roof."

No man ever made a success of life in any spot or place who was looking for a chance to escape the "daily grind."

Everything comes to him who hustles while he waits.

Thomas Mann always worked on each book for a very long time. Even when the manuscript was supposedly ready, he continued to work on it. When he kept on making changes in *Magic Mountain*, his publisher finally called and wailed, "We'll never get this book out. You have been working on it for eternity."

"After all," was the writer's calm reply, "I'm writing it for eternity."

"Ah, so that's the oldest inhabitant?" asked the city man. "A venerable figure, truly. How do you account for his having lived all these years?"

"Well," a trifle acid was the landlord's reply. "I guess it's because he's never done anything else."

Beware of the little thread of laziness.

The Little Thread of Selfishness

Another little thread that binds big men is the thread of selfishness. Paul said, "We then that are strong ought to bear the infirmities of the weak, and not to please ourselves" (Romans 15:1).

Selfishness is a sort of slow poison. One dose leads to another until the system becomes so saturated with it that one's whole life becomes bitter and disappointing. Larger doses are tried in desperation, but they fail to produce the desired results. The end is disappointing.

English theologian W. E. Sangster has made his point vividly with an anecdote from the sinking of the *Titanic*. Just after ten o'clock on the night of April 14, 1912, the largest vessel then afloat crashed into an iceberg in mid-Atlantic and, four hours later, ended its maiden voyage on the ocean floor. Books and movies have told the story of those frightening four hours: the heroism of the captain, officers, and crew; the bandmaster who played "Nearer, My God, to Thee," while getting into his life jacket.

Then comes the story—less moving but not less interesting.

A certain woman, who had been allotted a place in one of the boats, asked if she might run back to her stateroom and was given the permission to go. She hurried along the corridors already tilting at a dangerous angle. Money and costly gems littered the floor. Some who snatched at their jewelry spilt it as they ran. In her own stateroom, she saw her treasures waiting to be picked up. She saw—and took no heed. Snatching at three oranges which she knew to be there, she ran to take her place in the boat.

"That little incident is instructive," the writer continues. "An hour before it would have seemed incredible to that woman that she could prefer a crate of oranges to one small diamond, but Death boarded the

Titanic and, with one blast of his awful breath, all values were transformed. Precious things become worthless; worthless things become precious. Oranges were worth more than diamonds."

Selfish men have a warped concept of values. This little thread of selfishness has destroyed many big men.

An unselfish man is one who is interested in others. He is one who will listen to and appreciate another man's interests.

A friend tells of an old gentleman he met on a train.

"Have you any grandchildren?" the old fellow asked.

"Yes," my friend said.

Then the fellow went to another passenger and said, "Have you any grandchildren?"

"Yes," was the reply.

So he went to another, "Have you any grandchildren?"

"No."

"Move over," said the old gentleman happily. "I want to tell you all about mine."

Many never get a word in. The most important word in their vocabulary is the little word *I*. This is a sure sign of selfishness.

The minister was gathering data for the funeral service, and he inquired as to the last words of the deceased man. While the widow pondered, her little son piped up and said, "Last words? Pop never got in no last words; Mom was with him to the end."

A *bore* is a man who talks so much about himself that you don't have a chance to talk about yourself. We all need to pray the preacher's prayer:

Lord, to preach, give me the stuff;
Then nudge me when I've said enough.

Two men, riding in a sleigh while a blizzard was raging, were almost frozen and despaired of reaching their destination in safety. Suddenly, they came upon another traveler who had fallen in the snow and was nearing death from the terrific cold. One of the men suggested that they try to help the stranger. The other refused, stating it would jeopardize their own lives. He insisted on proceeding, but the first man decided to get out and do what he could for the fallen traveler. So the latter set to work at the task of restoring the fallen man's circulation and getting him to his feet.

After a long while, he responded to the massaging and in the process of saving another, the rescuer himself was saved. The man who refused to leave the sleigh was found farther down the road, frozen to death.

The best way to keep alive spiritually is to become vitally concerned about helping others. In so doing, we not only bring blessings to others but our own lives are enriched. The hand that is extended to give help to others is also extended to receive help from God.

On one occasion, General Booth wanted to send a message by wire or cable to every Salvation Army post in the world. His treasurer said, "General, telegrams are costly." General Booth replied, "I can send a message in one word." One of his staff said, "What is the magic word?" The general replied, "Others." The message was sent: "Others."

The quest for self, for wealth, for knowledge, when selfishly pursued, is a course that soon exhausts itself and is barren of peace. Dives was rich, but he wasn't happy. Faust had knowledge, but the devil had a mortgage on his soul. The prodigal son was having a great time, but he was moving toward want and the loss of money and friends.

Emerson said, "The selfish man suffers more from his selfishness than he from whom that selfishness withholds some important benefit."

Dickens's Scrooge is literature's immortal personification of selfishness. He is the arch-miser of the story *A Christmas Carol*. The man's grasping greed wrinkled his face and lent a squeak to his voice. One day he saw the ghost of his old partner bound with a chain made of cash boxes, keys, padlocks, ledgers, deeds, and ponderous purses wrought in steel. "You are fettered," ventured Scrooge, trembling all over.

"I wear the chains I forged in life," replied the ghost. "I made it link by link, and yard by yard. Is its pattern strange to you? Perhaps you do not know," continued the ghost, "that you carry a coil yourself. It was full and heavy as this seven Christmas Eves ago. You have laboured on it since. Its links are large and lusty today."

Dickens thus speaks to us that selfishness will bring its reward and that the solitude of Ebenezer Scrooge is a perpetual warning from the leaves of fiction.

Beware lest we become bound by the little thread of selfishness.

The Little Thread of Ingratitude

Another little ugly thread that binds men is the little thread of ingratitude.

Perhaps one of the ugliest known sins is that of ingratitude. Even in children it brings a mar of ugliness. No matter how beautiful the face, it can never compensate for the imperfection of ingratitude. Likewise, a very plain person can add to his beauty by a spirit of gratitude.

James Farley tells of this experience: "Not long ago in my mail I received a request from a college student, a young man who said he was writing a thesis on government. He knew of my background in politics and asked me to fill out a questionnaire.

"There were at least forty questions, and some of them called for detailed and complex answers. I was quite busy, but believing that any interest in government should be encouraged, I sat down with my secretary and dictated a long reply.

"It took most of the afternoon, but I finally sent it off with the little glow of satisfaction that comes from completing an arduous and voluntary task.

"I looked forward to receiving from this young man some acknowledgement as to whether I had helped him or not. But I have yet to hear from him to this day.

"I told myself that it was a matter of no great consequence and to put it out of my mind; forget it. But, obviously, since I am writing about it now, I didn't forget it. I didn't forget it because I was disappointed.

"The truth is, ingratitude hurts everyone. It also hurts the person who fails to show appreciation because he may make an enemy where he could have kept a friend.

"Simply feeling gratitude is not enough; it has to be demonstrated, one way or another. Perhaps the boy was appreciative, but, if so, his appreciation is wasted because he never told me. Two simple words, *thank you,* could have made all the difference."

A real New England tightwad, desperately ill, was visited one afternoon by the local pastor who was most solicitous. The tightwad was really touched. "Help me get well, Reverend Martin," he muttered, "and I will donate twenty-five thousand dollars to the new building fund."

The pastor smiled benignly and said he would pray for his speedy recovery. After three weeks the skinflint was back on his feet, fully recovered. The clergyman thereupon made numerous attempts to get in touch with the man to remind him of his promise. Finally, he cornered him in a store one afternoon and firmly reminded him of his words. "You promised," he said, "to give twenty-five thousand dollars if you recovered your health. Where is it?"

The skinflint was amazed. "I did?" he said in astonishment. "Well, that gives you a rough idea of how sick I was."

It is well and proper for us to express our gratitude to others. Sometimes we sound a little foolish, but the message is understood.

A lady said to me one time, "You are surely a wonderful preacher. You know, we really didn't know what sin was until you came." I think I understood what she meant. I *hope* that I did!

Paul wrote to the Thessalonians, "In every thing give thanks . . ." (1 Thessalonians 5:18). This is more than good advice. It is a command. Christians should make every day Thanksgiving Day. When a Christian is unthankful, he is guilty of positive sin. It is the sin of disobedience.

Three things are necessary if we are to be perpetually grateful. *First,* we must not limit our gratitude for the pleasant things only. The bitter as well as the sweet are included in Paul's "everything." Our dark experiences are as necessary as the bright ones. The medicine that cures is often bitter. We are thankful when success crowns our efforts. Paul practiced his own advice. He was imprisoned, whipped, stoned, slandered, and finally killed. They killed his body, but not the thanksgiving in his heart. He cried, "Hallelujah" to the end.

Second, our gratitude must not be limited to one realm of blessings. For what then should we be grateful? Start at the bottom. We should be grateful for the common, everyday things: food, clothes, friends, country, churches, loved ones, Bible, and so on.

Let us go a rung higher. We should be grateful for salvation through Christ. This is God's great gift to us— never earned, never deserved, but freely given.

Let us go still higher. We should be grateful for Jesus who is now at the right hand of God interceding for us. Through Him we go to God, the Father.

Let us go still higher. We should be grateful for God's providence. God has assured us that all things work together for our good. God has so commanded. This includes the sunshine experiences and the lonely walk through the night of reverses and sorrow.

Let us go to the top. We should be thankful for the hope beyond. Heaven is our destination. The sorrows of this life form the background for the brightness of the Father's house.

Third, we must not be discouraged in our efforts to reach this goal. It is not attained in a moment. It means a long, hard struggle with self and environment. We will lose many a battle, but if we persist, we will win the war.

To help us attain perpetual gratitude, keep in mind four suggestions:

1. Maintain a real, vital faith in God. This is a faith that is stronger than sight, a faith that holds when we cannot understand, indeed, a faith that will not let go.

2. Remember that our achievements are not ours but God's. We must not thank ourselves for Christian achievement. Selfishness must die out in us before gratitude reigns. We must be careful never to wear a crown of praise that belongs to Christ. When we have done our best, we are still unprofitable servants.

3. Beware of allowing the blessings of others to make us despise our own. King Saul appreciated the praise of the people until they began to praise David. We appreciate the daisy in our hand until we see the rose in our neighbor's hand. Our little cottage is wonderful until we see our neighbor's mansion.

4. We must be careful to express gratitude. Mary was so consumed by her gratitude to Jesus that she forgot herself when she anointed Him. The man of Gadara, whom Jesus healed, fell before Him.

Next time you feel ungrateful, fall on your face and ask God to forgive you for your sin of ingratitude.

Paul said, "Give thanks in all circumstances . . ." (1 Thessalonians 5:18 RSV). Paul was a master of the fine art of appreciation. It is a thrill to open the Bible and walk through the pages to see the radiant souls whose faces shine with the joy of gratitude. Of all these giants, Paul is recognized as the master of gratitude.

The Bible is crystal clear in the matter of gratitude.

Mark Twain once said, "Most people are bothered about the passages of Scripture which they cannot understand; but, as for me, I have always noticed that the passages which trouble me most are those which I do understand."

Bishop Fulton J. Sheen said, "The proud man counts his newpaper clippings—the humble man, his blessings."

A miserly banker lost a wallet containing quite a bit of money. An honest man happened to find it and advertised for the loser. The miser claimed it, and the finder, being satisfied that it belonged to him, cheerfully returned it to the loser. He, thereupon, counted the contents several times to the disgust of the finder, who indignantly inquired, "Isn't the amount right?"

"Yes, sir," the miser replied, "but you must remember that you had it over a month. What about some interest?"

Seneca wrote, "If I only have the will to be grateful, I am so."

Cicero calls gratitude the mother of virtues, the most capital of all duties, and uses the words *grateful* and *good* as synonymous terms, inseparable, united in the same character.

He that calls a man ungrateful, sums up all the evil of which one can be guilty.

Colonial merchant Timothy Dexter was right when he said, "An ungrateful man is like a hog under a tree eating acorns but never looking up to see where they come from."

John Bunyan carried it further when he wrote, "He that forgets his friend is ungrateful to him; but he that forgets his Saviour is unmerciful to himself."

"I hate ingratitude more in man than lying, vainness, babbling, drunkenness, or any taint of vice, whose strong corruption inhabits our frail look." So wrote Shakespeare.

This little thread of ingratitude binds many big men to the block of misery.

Beware of the little threads that bind big men.

The little thread of jealousy.

The little thread of discouragement.

The little thread of laziness.

The little thread of selfishness.

The little thread of ingratitude.

2

The Secret of Real Beauty

And it came to pass when Moses came down from mount Sinai (with the two tables of testimony in Moses' hand, when he came down from the mount) that Moses wist not that the skin of his face shone, while he talked with him.

Exodus 34:29

American women spend more than two billion dollars a year on beauty aids. Many a girl would rather have beauty than brains, because she knows that the average man can see better than he can think. But, no longer do women have a monopoly on the intricate secrets of beauty. Alas, men have fallen prey.

A friend of mine gave me this little story. A preacher had two sons. The small boys were watching a popular program on television. Suddenly on came a commercial showing twin brothers in a high-speed motorboat. One of the twins was driving the speedboat and apparently had not used the particular hair preparation. His hair was all tangled and unruly. His brother was in the backseat with his arm around a beautiful young lady. His hair was well combed, and apparently he had used this miracle preparation. One of the preacher's boys watching the commercial said, "I'll tell you one thing: I'll never use that stuff on my hair."

"Why not?" asked the father.

The lad looked up at his dad and said, "Who wants to kiss a girl when you can drive a boat?"

An old mountaineer was walking along the highway when he happened to find a mirror. He had never seen a mirror and was completely ignorant as to its properties. As he looked at it and saw his reflection, he remarked, "Well, if it isn't a picture of my old pappy." He took the mirror home and put it in the barn.

One day his wife was out in the barn and found the mirror. She looked into it and saw her own reflection. With great consternation she said, "So that's the old bag my husband has been running around with."

Perhaps the way we look is an indication of the way we think. A preacher, driving out west, stopped in a moment of misguided compassion to pick up a hitch-hiker. Braking at an intersection, he asked his unwashed passenger if any traffic was coming from the right. "Only a dog, man," was the reply.

Pulling out on the highway, they were run over by a large vehicle. When the preacher woke up in the hospital, turned and saw the hitchhiker, encased in a body cast, occupying the other bed in the room, he screamed, "What kind of dog were you talking about?"

"It was just a dog, man—a Greyhound," was the non-chalant reply.

What is real beauty?

The poet Francis Quarles, in one of his writings, had this to say about beauty: "Socrates called beauty a short-lived tyranny; Plato, a privilege of nature; Theophrastus, a silent cheat; Theocritus, a delightful prejudice; Carneades, a solitary kingdom; Aristotle, that it was better than all the letters of recommendation in the world; Homer, that it was a glorious gift of nature; and Ovid, that it was a favor bestowed by the gods."

When Moses came down from Mount Sinai where he had been with God for forty days and forty nights, the Bible records, that "Moses wist not that the skin of his face shone."

It has been said, "True Christian excellence shines naturally like the sun, not for the effect, but because it cannot keep from shining." It was so with the face of Moses. But whenever a Christian's grace becomes self-conscious, it loses its charm. It is like an Alpine flower brought from the lonely mountain peak where it blushes unseen. Planted in the public garden, it loses its beauty and fragrance and becomes a mere weed.

You cannot handle a butterfly's wings without rubbing off its delicate mealy dust. And, so, you cannot handle admiringly your own Christian virtue without impairing its tender loveliness.

The fountain of beauty is in the heart, and every generous thought illustrates the walls of your chamber. Moses gives to us the secret of real beauty.

Among women the biological factors which tend to cause the greatest difficulty are the changes in outward appearance. Women who have used sexual attractiveness and physical beauty as a means of achieving domination, security, or social status, instead of developing real charm and skill in human relations and a positive self-evaluation for deeper qualities of worth, view the biological process of aging as a special threat. The arbitrary standards of physical beauty and the mentality that attractiveness is reserved for youth heightens the threat of aging. There is, in fact, a beauty which is intrinsic to each age. There is a beauty inherent in six or sixty as well as sixteen. As a matter of fact, the real and permanent qualities which make for personal attractiveness are largely reflective of character.

Many volumes have been written on the evidences of Christianity, but the supreme evidence of Christianity is a Christian. A Christian is the Gospel written on heart and mind and bound in flesh and blood. We indeed are living Epistles, known and read of all men. The unsaved world is looking, not to the Scriptures, but to the people of God for a demonstration of the saving power of Jesus Christ.

The lighthouse keeper sitting by his flaming lamp can see scarce a yard beyond his door, but far off on the deep the storm-tossed mariner sees the light and by its rays is guided to a safe harbor. Even so is the true Christian sending a guiding light into the world's darkness.

Without a theological discussion I call your attention to an illustration of real beauty. "Moses wist not that the skin of his face shone."

What Is the Source of This Real Beauty?

Standing in the presence of a man like Moses, with his face radiant with the glory of God, we ask, how did he obtain this beauty?

It came after long and patient service for God. The light was not on his face as he lay in the ark of bulrushes. It was not transmitted to him by Amram and Jochebed, godly people though they were. It was not there as he pleaded the cause of enslaved Israel.

Moses had to spend forty years in Midian, learning that God's time was better than his time and God's method was better than his method.

He had to face the fiery Pharaoh and demand the liberty of the Hebrews. He had to lead a stiffnecked and perverse people to the foot of Sinai before self was so obliterated that his only thought was to do the will of Jehovah. The unconscious beauty of a consecrated life is not a fruit that ripens in a day.

An old legend tells us that when God made the birds, He did not give them wings, and they went hopping about on the ground. One day He asked them to become burden bearers for Him and placed two little burdens on the shoulders of each little bird.

Day by day they carried their loads and at last the burdens became wings. That which first pressed them down toward the earth became the means by which they mounted toward the sky. The cross which at first crushed our Lord to the earth has become the throne of His external glory.

This beauty came from a close personal communion with God. In the mountain Moses talked face-to-face with Jehovah as a friend talks with a friend.

Among the people in the rural districts of England, it was a popular belief that the secret of female beauty was to be found in bathing the face in the morning and evening dew of the first day of May. Early in the morning, before the daystar began to grow dim, the maiden would go out and gather the dew in her hands and bathe her face. And again when the evening star appeared, she would repeat the process. Of course, that was only a foolish superstition, but the secret of spiritual beauty is to bathe the soul in morning and evening communion with God.

A dear old lady was asked what she used to make her complexion so beautiful and her whole being so bright and attractive. She answered in short:

> I use for my lips, truth;
> I use for my voice, kindness;
> I use for my eyes, compassion;
> I use for my hands, charity;
> I use for my figure, uprightness;
> I use for my heart, love;
> I use for any who do not like me, prayer.

I wonder what would happen if we used this makeup.

We become like the people whom we love and with whom we have close personal association. It is not a mere fancy that discovers a likeness between husband and wife. After years of personal communion in which they think and act alike, there comes to be a likeness in their faces, for our faces mirror the Spirit that occupies the heart.

The Bible describes a beautiful person when it speaks of "the fruit of the Spirit is love, joy, peace, longsuffering, gentleness, goodness, faith, Meekness, temperance . . ." (Galatians 5:22, 23).

There is a Chinese proverb which reads: "If there is righteousness in the heart, there is beauty in the character. If there is beauty in the character, there will be harmony in the home. If there is harmony in the home, there will be order in the nation. If there is order in the nation, there will be peace in the world."

> There is beauty in the forest
> When the trees are green and fair,
> There is beauty in the meadow
> When wild flowers scent the air.
> There is beauty in the sunlight
> And the soft blue beams above.
> Oh, the world is full of beauty
> When the heart is full of love.
>   AUTHOR UNKNOWN

This beauty comes in connection with intense sacrifice for others.

A few days ago this little story came to my attention. A young father, pushing a baby carriage, seemed quite unperturbed by the wails emerging from it. "Easy now, Albert," he said quietly, "control yourself. Keep calm." Another howl rang out. "Now, now, Albert," murmured the parent, "Keep your temper."

A young mother passing by remarked, "I must congratulate you." Smilingly she said, "You know just how to talk to babies calmly and gently." She patted the youngster on the head and cooed, "What's bothering you, Albert?"

"No, no," cried the father. "His name is Harold; I'm Albert."

Measure thy life by loss instead of gain;
Not by the wine drunk, but by the wine poured
   forth,
For love's strength standeth in love's sacrifice,
And those who suffer most hath most to give.

                                  AUTHOR UNKNOWN

If there will be room for regret in heaven, it will not be because we sacrificed so much here for the Gospel's sake, but rather that we did not sacrifice more.

"When I got home last night," the young husband said, "my wife greeted me with a hug and a kiss. She had a delicious dinner ready. Afterward, she wouldn't let me help her with the dishes, but made me sit in the living room and read the paper."

"And how did you like her new outfit?" his friend asked.

"Why do you wear those rubber boots on a hot day?" a small boy asked a man who was working on an electric line. "Do you think it might rain today?"

The man smiled at the boy and replied, "No, sonny, I wear these to save me from electric shock. Electricity does not pass through rubber very well, and one of the funny things about electricity is that it can't get into a person unless it can get out again!"

What a perfect explanation of love. It can't dwell in the human heart unless you are willing to let it out again. It must have expression or it will die.

It is great to live; it is greater to live for others; it is greatest to live for God.

The final step in Moses' upward climb was an intense zeal for the glory of God. This is the mountain crest of consecration. To reveal the glory of God is the supreme mission of every redeemed soul.

What Is the Effect of Real Beauty?

It made him conspicuous. Moses wist not that the skin of his face shown, but it was plain to everyone else in the camp. The world will always be conscious of unconscious beauty. This beauty and love affects others. Think about these lines:

> I love you, not only for what you are,
> But for what I am when I am with you.
> I love you, not only for what you have made of
>   yourself,
> But for what you are making of me.
>
> ELIZABETH BARRETT BROWNING

The old artists always painted their saints with halos about their heads, because they would have us understand that the beauty of holiness is visible to all except the wearer. In the old dispensations the high priest wore on his forehead a signet upon which was engraved, "Holiness unto the LORD." It was worn where all except the priest could see it. It made him humble.

J. D. Grey, the longtime pastor of the First Baptist Church of New Orleans, often admonishes young preachers with "Your halo is too tight." Real saints are hardly aware of this quality in themselves.

There is a loud-mouthed, blatant kind of holiness in

the world today, and it is always boasting of its superior beauty. It has denunciation for all except itself and vaunts its own preeminence. At best it is but polished brass trying to pass itself off as gold.

Let us remember that the garment of humility and patience is made "while you wait."

It is said of Dr. Will H. Houghton, late president of Moody Bible Institute in Chicago, that he was truly great because he was truly humble.

Sometimes the preacher can "get his foot in a lard bucket" not by lying but by exaggerating some facts. One preacher was so given to this practice, until one of his deacons discussed this matter of his exaggerating. The preacher was very contrite and asked for the help of the deacon in keeping straight on the matter. It was agreed that at any time the preacher exaggerated too much, the deacon would let out with a low whistle which was a signal to the preacher to "cool it." One Sunday the pastor was preaching on Samson's tying the tails of the foxes together and setting the Philistines' field on fire. He said, "Those foxes had long tails; why, would you believe it—their tails were thirty feet long."

The deacon let out a subdued whistle. The preacher backed up and said, "Come to think of it, I don't think their tails were more than twenty feet long." Another whistle came from the deacon.

"Well, I'll be honest with you, I don't think the tails were but ten feet long." Still another whistle came from the deacon. At this juncture the preacher became exasperated and said to the deacon, "Now you can go on whistling your head off, but I'm not going to cut their tails another foot!"

True holiness is like wheat, the riper it becomes, the lower it bends its head.

This beauty made Moses fearless.

Two men were visiting before a banquet when one said to the other, "That woman over there is the ugliest woman I have ever seen in my life. I wonder who she is?"

The other man said, "Why, that's my wife."

Surprised, the other man replied, "You think she is ugly; you ought to see my wife."

There is no place for fear in the consecrated life of a Christian. There must be humility, but there must be no halting. Like Moses we may have to stand alone but, like him, we will find that one with God is always a majority.

> The tumult and the shouting dies;
> The Captains and the Kings depart:
> Still stands Thine ancient sacrifice,
> An humble and a contrite heart.
>   RUDYARD KIPLING

A fine young man came into his uncle's office and said, "Uncle, I am deeply in love with a beautiful young lady. How can I know what she really thinks of me?"

The wise uncle said, "Marry her, my boy, marry her."

Finally, spiritual beauty makes him victorious. Moses was victorious over himself. He was victorious over every opposing force and saw the golden calf destroyed and the people brought back to their allegiance to Jehovah. He brought the whole nation to its knees. Remember, we can never be spiritually effective until we are spiritually beautiful.

Do we really want our faces to shine? If we do, then there is an old Egypt to be abandoned; there is a Pharaoh to be faced; there is a mountain to be climbed; and there is a face-to-face living with God.

We need to pray with the Psalmist, "And let the beauty of the Lord our God be upon us: and establish thou the work of our hands upon us . . ." (Psalms 90:17).

3

My Philosophy of Life

For me to live is Christ, and to die is gain.
                                    Philippians 1:21

This seems to be Paul's philosophy of life. English Clergyman Dr. John Henry Jowett says, "There are three cardinal words in this passage—*me, live, Christ.* The middle term, *live,* is defined in the union of the other two. If you put two carbon electrodes into proper relationship and turn on the electricity, the result will be a light of brilliant intensity." So the Apostle says that if I join "me" to "Christ," I shall have life in its fullness. It will be true and genuine life.

There are many great philosophies of life.

The Greek philosophy—"know thyself."
The Roman philosophy—"control thyself."
The Christian philosophy—"give thyself."

Perhaps it would be well to name a few more philosophies.

The pig-pen philosophy—"get all you can as quickly as you can."
The bingo philosophy—"get all you can for nothing."
The main-street philosophy—"do all that others do."

Seneca wrote: "Philosophy is the art and law of life, and it teaches us what to do in all cases, and, like good marksmen, to hit the white at any distance."

True philosophy invents nothing; it merely establishes and describes what is.

Plutarch said, "Philosophy is the art of living."

Aristotle said, "Philosophy is the science which considers truth."

Everyone has a philosophy of life. Whether he realizes it or not, he preaches it every day. Others recognize our philosophy of life whether we do or not.

Jesus said, ". . . I am come that they might have life, and that they might have it more abundantly" (John 10:10).

Abundant life is a wonderful thing. It should be enjoyed by all. However, there are some people who are more afraid of life than death.

Dr. Joseph Cook describes life this way:

Tender teens;
　Teachable twenties;
　　Tireless thirties;
　　　Fiery forties;
　　　　Forcible fifties;
　　　　　Serious sixties;
　　　　　　Sacred seventies;
　　　　　　　Aching eighties;
　　　　　　　　Shortening breath;
　　　　　　　　　Death;
　　　　　　　　　　The sod;
　　　　　　　　　　　God.

When I was in college, a friend gave me a book entitled, *The Key to Success*. I read it, then I looked up the author to find out what he had done. I discovered that he probably had the key to success, but he himself never found the keyhole. To succeed in life, one must have both a key and a keyhole.

In an address to the undergraduates of Harvard University, Theodore Roosevelt said, "Education is the development of all one's ordinary powers to an extraordinary degree of efficiency."

Bishop Edgar Blake once told of a fine young man in New England who fell in love with the pastor's daughter and asked for her hand in marriage. The father refused to consent to the marriage. Said the father, "I refused to give my consent—not because I have any objection to you, but rather because I know you cannot live with my daughter."

The young man was visibly surprised, "Why, is she not a Christian?" "Oh, yes," said the father, "my daughter is a Christian, but when you have lived as long as I have, you will know that there are people whom God can live with but no one else can."

A very effective preacher and close friend of mine for many years is Dr. Angel Martinez. One of my favorite stories about Angel took place many years ago when he was a very young ministerial student at Baylor University. They had taken Angel out of San Antonio but they had not taken San Antonio out of Angel.

He simply loved to eat Mexican red-hot chili peppers. He had been eating them all his life and ate them like peanuts.

After dinner in the home of a deacon, Angel ate a few of the little balls of fire. The deacon noticed it and asked for a handful of them, assuring Angel he could eat anything a young minister could. The deacon swallowed about a dozen of them.

Three gallons of water later, the flaming deacon exclaimed, "I've heard many, many preachers preach about hell-fire, but you are the first one I've ever known who carries samples with him!"

As I look out upon the sea of this world, I realize the importance of recognizing one's philosophy of life. With this in mind, be patient with me, as I give you my philosophy of life.

There are three foundation stones upon which I will build my philosophy of life.

This is a Purposeful World

In the beginning God created. Occasionally a person should rethink the foundation stones of creation. We are beneath the clouds, but God is above them. Man is in the shadows, but Christ is in the light. There is no mystery to God. He is the ruler of this creation. God holds the scepter of all power. Man can go just as far as God will permit him to go and not one step further. This knowledge of divine truth will determine one's conduct and philosophy of life.

There is a purpose to this world. Henry Ward Beecher, the famous preacher, said, "The heavens and the earth alike speak of God, and the great natural world is but another Bible which clasps and binds the written one; for nature and grace are one—grace, the heart of the flower, and nature, its surrounding petals."

God made this world. He planned it, and He understands it. He has a purpose for it. A few years ago there was a popular song that revealed this truth. The title of the song was, "He's Got the Whole World in His Hands." This world was not flung off into space to drift aimlessly.

Yet, little man is puzzled by this world. This process of living is a dangerous endeavor. As a matter of fact, very few get out of it alive.

Some make the mistake of thinking the present picture is permanent. Nothing earthly is permanent. It may be slow, but it's still moving.

Outside a monastery in Tibet, two venerable lamas sunned themselves day after day, rarely talking, engaged in deep meditation. On February 14, one lama stopped stroking his beard long enough to remark, "Life, my friend, is like a well." The other said nothing until March 9, when he suddenly rumbled, "Why is life like a well?" On April 22, the first lama shrugged his shoulders and commented, "All right, have it your own way. Life isn't like a well."

The movement may be for the better or worse.

The young daughter was very boisterous, and her father wanted her quiet so he could read. He clipped a large map from the paper, tore it into bits like a jigsaw puzzle, and told the daughter to sit down and put the map together again. This, he thought, would keep her occupied for several hours.

The little girl was delighted and took the handful of torn paper. In just a little while she was back, with the map all neatly arranged and perfectly put together. "See, Daddy. Here it is."

Her father was much surprised. "Well, how in the world did you do it so quickly?" he asked.

"Well, you see," she replied, "there is a big picture of a man on the other side, and I just put him together and turned it over. You see, Daddy, if the man is right, the world will come out all right, too."

Many times man will think that the failure of civilization is the failure of God.

Toward the close of his life, Sir Isaac Newton, who discovered the law of gravity and contributed much to man's total knowledge, likened himself to a child picking up pebbles on the seashore, while the vast ocean of undiscovered truth swept out and away from him. The closer we draw to Christ, the more we become aware of our un-Christlikeness.

Man thinks the cruelties of nations do not harmonize with the love of God. Men do what they want to do.

A few years ago in Dallas, Texas, Dwight L. Lowelling, beloved apostle of charity, died. During ten years of work in behalf of bums, tramps, and transients, he befriended twenty thousand. Only five of the twenty thousand attended his funeral held at the Gaston Avenue Baptist Church. Friends, who expected to see the church overrun by shabbily dressed men to whom he had supplied food and sleeping quarters only through superhuman efforts, were shocked when they viewed the congregation. Only five out of twenty thousand whom he had helped and befriended came to pay a tribute of love.

The human heart hasn't changed much since only one out of ten lepers returned to express gratitude for cleansing. But, we have the Master's word that whosoever giveth a cup of cold water in His name shall in no wise lose his reward.

Elizabeth Barrett Browning said, "The world may sound no trumpets, ring no bells—The Book of Life the shining record tells."

This world in which I live is a purposeful world.

This Is an Imperfect World

This is an imperfect world because it is made up of imperfect people. During this lifetime, we will never reach that utopia of which we dream. Like a mirage of a lake on the desert floor, we'll never reach the cool water in this life. On this side of the Divine, there is no perfection.

Although there is no perfection, some have made great strides in seeking improvement. Angelo Siciliano, better known as Charles Atlas, is a most encouraging example. At sixteen he was a ninety-seven-pound runt and a common victim of bullies' rough stuff. But while visiting the

Brooklyn Museum, he got a vision of strength. He saw the statues of Apollo and Hercules. He was told that young Greek athletes had served as models for the statues. That very day he began exercising according to instructions he found in a newspaper. Sarcasm and ridicule did not daunt him. He didn't give up. Later, he invented his own exercises. He became the mighty Atlas, and it was said that he was: "the possessor of the true classic physique, a blend of Hercules and Apollo"; "the world's most perfectly developed man." Why was he able to achieve this? Because his feeling of inferiority motivated him to great effort.

There are no perfect churches. Every now and then someone feels compelled to inform me of all that is wrong with the church. After he finishes his long list of faults, I am prepared to add some that he had never thought of. We preachers preach many sermons on what is wrong with the church, but it is time for us to preach a sermon on what is right with the church. While attending Southwestern Baptist Theological Seminary, I had a professor who constantly reminded us that we would never have a perfect church. He would smile and say, "If it were perfect, they never would have called you." The church is made up of imperfect people.

A man had been around from church to church, trying to find a congenial congregation, and finally stopped in a little church just as the congregation read with the minister: "We have left undone those things which we ought to have done; and we have done those things which we ought not to have done." The man dropped into a pew with a sigh of relief. "Thank goodness," he observed.

"I've found my crowd at last!"

Recently, I met a pastor who told me he was resigning from his church because of illness—his people were sick of him.

One layman said, "There are two schools of thought about our pastor. People either dislike him or hate him."

No nation is perfect. On the monument of Governor William Bradford of Plymouth Colony is inscribed in Latin, "What our fathers with so much difficulty secured do not basely relinquish."

That admonition from a great Christian is a challenge to conserve our religious heritage, the liberty, convictions, and heroic character that make us a nation.

We have become a slack-backed generation. What our times need above all else is sturdy souls who know themselves to be free sons of God in pursuit of His will.

In all the appraisals of America there is one point in agreement—America is different. There may be disagreement as to the causes that produced such a strange member of the family of nations, but the fact itself cannot be challenged.

America is strangely different from all other nations both past and present. The difference is to be found in the soul of America—the soul of America is God. Although America is not perfect, it is the greatest nation on the face of the earth. It affords more opportunities to its people than any nation from the beginning of recorded history. But many times we become disgusted with what we see.

A rather old-fashioned fellow watching some teenagers engaged in a modern dance, said to the bystander, "It's terrible the way they dress today. Just look at that girl with the cigarette, sloppy, unkempt hair and tight pants."

The bystander replied, "That's not a girl—it's a boy, and he's my son."

The man said, "Oh, excuse me, sir, I didn't know you were his father."

"I'm not," said the other, "I'm his mother."

There are no perfect men or women. The Bible makes this crystal clear by saying, "For all have sinned, and come short of the glory of God" (Romans 3:23).

John Wesley was asked what he meant by attainment of perfection in his life. His answer was, "It meant nothing more than loving God with all our heart and serving Him with all our strength."

The cardinal was in his chauffeur-driven limousine which was going down Michigan Boulevard at excessive speed. He was stopped by a traffic officer, who took out his book to give the driver a ticket. He had only wet his pencil, however, when the prelate in his churchly robes opened the rear door and inquired, "What's the trouble?" "Oh, no trouble at all, Your Eminence," the policeman said. "I was warnin' the driver that there is a Protestant cop on the next corner."

There is no perfect marriage. Two lovers walk down the street. She trips; he murmurs, "Careful, sweet." Now wed, they tread that selfsame street. She trips; he growls, "Pick up your feet."

A little girl asked her school chum how she liked her

new father. "Fine," said Birdie. "We liked him, too," said Beatrice. "We had him last year."

A friend declares that he and his wife never have arguments. They reason things out in an amicable manner. There are times, however, he says, when their reasoning is so loud that the neighbors complain.

When a couple, married for many years, were asked by a reporter if they ever considered divorce, the wife answered thoughtfully, "Well, sometimes I have thought of killing him, but I never once considered divorce."

There are no perfect marriages.

During the reign of Bloody Mary, Queen of England, the saintly Bernard Gilpin was accused of heresy. Messengers were sent to apprehend him and to bring him to London for execution. Gilpin was informed of his peril but refused to escape. "All things work together for good," he said. On the trip to London, while under arrest, he fell and broke his leg. "Is that for the best?" one of the attendants jeeringly asked. "Yes, I believe so," the prisoner replied.

He was right. Before he was able to continue his journey to London, Queen Mary died, and instead of being burned at the stake, he returned home in triumph. God used a broken leg to save his life.

Walter Moore, the gifted preacher, loves to tell about a man who told Billy Sunday, "If you tell me where Cain got his wife, I'll believe your Gospel."

Sunday snapped back, "You won't be the first man who went to hell worrying about another man's wife."

This is an imperfect world!

This Purposeful, Imperfect World Houses the Crown of Creation—Man

> Animal nature, however perfect, is far from representing the human being in its completeness and is in truth but humanity's handmaid, made to serve and obey.
>
> POPE LEO XIII

Man is capable of faith. As the flower is before the fruit, so is faith before good works. Man is the only animal that smiles, sheds tears, and blushes.

Men are what women marry. They are divided into three classes: bachelors, husbands, and widowers. A bachelor is a man whose mind and soul are filled with suspicion. Husbands are of three varieties: prize, surprise, and consolation prize.

Making a husband out of a man is one of the highest arts known to civilization. It is a science, requiring patience, persistence, faith, hope, and charity.

If you flatter a man, you frighten him to death; if you don't, you bore him to death. If you permit him to make love to you, he gets tired of you in the end; if you don't, he gets tired of you in the beginning. If you believe all he tells you, he thinks you are foolish; if you don't, he gets mad and thinks you are a cynic. If you wear gay colors, rouge, and crazy clothes, he doubts that you have any brains; if you are modern, advanced, and intelligent, he doubts that you have a heart. If you are silly, he longs for a bright mate; if you are intelligent and brilliant, he longs for a playmate.

Oh, this strange creature, man!

Man is capable of hope.

Emerson said, "Hope writes the poetry of the boy, but memory that of the man. Man looks forward with smiles, but backward with sighs. Such is the wise providence of God. The cup of life is sweetness at the brim—the flavor is impaired as we drink deeper, and the dregs are made bitter that we may not struggle when it is taken from our lips."

Hope is the greatest of preachers. Rob a man of hope, and you pull the curtain on his life. He may fathom the abysmal depths to which he may fall or glimpse the sublime heights to which he may climb.

When we saturate ourselves with memories of the superb achievements of men and women of the past in the various realms of human endeavor, we are thrilled at the thought of the limitless possibilities for our lives. As we live in remembrance of these great ones of the ages, we gain confidence, determination, courage, patience, zeal, and joy.

Man is capable of love.

It is not decided that women love more than men, but it is indisputable that they love better.
THOMAS EDWARD DUBAY

In discovering my philosophy of life, I have made some resolutions. First, I will count on some disappointments. The sun will not shine every day. There will be the clouds, rain, and lightning. There will be mountaintop experiences, but there will also be the valley experiences. Among the ingredients of my life are some disappointments. I understand that the total product of life must have its disappointments.

Abraham Lincoln was asked how he felt after an unsuccessful election. He said he felt like a little boy who had stubbed his toe in the dark. He said that he was too old to cry, but it hurt too much to laugh.

I must not become discouraged. American political figure Chauncey Depew once paused to watch some kids in a sandlot baseball game. "What's the score, son?" he asked one of the participants. "It's twenty-eight to nothing agin' us right now," said the kid. "My," said Depew, "aren't you a bit discouraged?" "Discouraged, nothing," was the answer. "We ain't been to bat yet."

Vonda Kay Van Dyke was chosen Miss America in 1965. Miss Van Dyke was active in numerous musical groups, served on the school-newspaper staff, and was captain of the cheerleading squad. As an active church member, she sang in the choir and taught Sunday school. Vonda has climbed the ladder of success, step-by-step, and well knows the discipline it requires.

She is constantly sensitive and alert to all opportunities. She shares what she considers to be the most important gift of her life—her faith in God. In one of her statements she said, "Life can't make something out of you. You have to make something out of your life."

Second, I will not lose my poise. Nothing produces old age more quickly than the lack of self-control. If you are easily irritated, if you let people get on your nerves and have pet peeves, it is as devastating to good health as is an alcoholic spree. If it becomes a habit for you to blow up, lose your temper, and give into "nervous jags," you will soon be old, even if you are still in your teens. That sort of disposition will take its toll on your physical health and affect your mental, moral, and spiritual stability.

Horace Greeley, we are told, acquired the habit of almost perfect self-control. He did not allow any ordinary disturbance, disappointment or noise to irritate him. He would sit upon the curb of the street, use the top of his tall hat for a desk, and write an editorial for the New York *Tribune* while a great parade went by with bands playing loudly and the street was lined with shouting people.

Poise and calmness do much to help you and other people. They are contagious and act like oil on troubled water. Poise—the result of your refusing to be ruffled, avoiding emotional orgies, putting first things first— enables you to remain calm, composed, and able to use good judgment in any emergency.

Poise can be cultivated daily, at work, at play, and in the midst of your own family. In handling the small, disconcerting things of life, remember that a well-poised person might be compared to a sailboat, well-weighted by a deep keel, which quickly rights when it heels over in a gusty wind.

The best psychological keel you can have is the belief that God's hand is always on your shoulder, guiding you through shoals and darkness into a safe harbor.

An illiterate young mountain preacher had begun to preach with no formal equipment whatsoever. He was so uninstructed in the ways of the world that he found himself in the coils of the law without having committed a shockingly criminal act. It was, however, enough of a breach of the statutes to draw a one-year sentence in an Arkansas penitentiary. Afterward, he fled to Texas where he began to preach in a remote community under an assumed name, thinking his shady past would not be revealed.

However, on the first Sunday, as he was about to begin his sermon, he saw, sitting in a back pew, a former inmate in the penitentiary. He flipped over the pages of the Bible, as he said, "Brethren, under the influence of the Spirit, I'm going to haul off here and change my text."

Looking significantly at the back pew, he said, "My text is," and pretended to read, "if thou seest me and thinkest thou knowest me, say nothing, and I will see thee later."

There is nothing so destructive to health and happiness as the loss of control over one's emotions. Temperamental people become grouchy and old no matter what their age. Someone said that *temperamental* means "95 percent temper and 5 percent mental." The trouble with nervous, explosive people is that they are bestowing too much thought upon themselves.

Joe was having trouble getting up in the morning so his doctor prescribed some pills. Joe took them, slept well, and was awake before he heard the alarm. He took his time getting to the office, strolled in and said to the boss, "I didn't have a bit of trouble getting up this morning."

"That's fine," replied the boss, "but where were you yesterday?"

I will not become a victim of self-pity. Like the Psalmist, I will not lose my footing. Some men in a flashing moment have lost their future. An emotional explosion destroyed them.

I will not panic. This is a sure way to destroy usefulness. During these anxious times, I will keep my feet on the solid foundation. As the old hymn goes, "I shall not be moved."

I will guard against being cynical. Cynicism is nothing but idealism gone sour in the face of frustration. Have you ever wished, when unkind remarks were being tossed about, that you could close your ears and not have to hear such things?

Well, the woodchuck can do just that. Of course, he doesn't shut his ears to keep from hearing conversation. But he spends a great deal of his time digging the tunnels in which he and his family live and in which they take refuge from their natural enemies. While he is digging, often three feet or more below the surface, his ears would soon become filled with dirt if he could not close them. So nature has wisely provided Mr. Chuck with muscles he can use to close his ears tightly.

When we hear too much we are apt to become cynical. I want my life to be built on the positive note.

My third resolution is, I will pitch my life on a long-range faith. Life is measured not so much by its longevity as by its intensity. Victor Hugo said, "Winter is on my head, but eternal spring is in my heart." If you have the spirit of youth, with its courage and enthusiasm, you are young.

A useful life is a long-range project. It must be planned and then constructed. The foundation must be laid before the superstructure goes up. Right will win. The eternal promises of God are true. A philosopher sees less on his tiptoes than a Christian sees on his knees.

Lloyd George, in one of his lighter moments, said that "tranquility is never a philosophy or a policy. It is simply a great yawn."

Fourth, I will play for keeps. This life now is all that I have with which to work. What I do with it, I must do now. I am a bit of eternity. Since I am important in the eyes of my Creator, I will not disappoint Him.

Upon this life depends eternity. This is my philosophy of life.

4

The Half-baked

. . . Ephraim is a cake not turned.

Hosea 7:8

The ancients were famous feeders and brought the culinary art well-nigh to perfection. These ancients did not have the quick packaged goods that we do today.

Two cannibals met in a hut. One was tearing out pictures of men, women, and children from a magazine, stuffing them into his mouth, and eating them.

"Tell me," said the other, "is that dehydrated stuff any good?"

The office of chief baker was one of responsibility and peril, for while Pharaoh could forgive and restore to office the chief butler who had failed in the discharge of

69

his duties, he executed the chief baker. Possibly the man's poor cooking had caused the Pharaoh an attack of dyspepsia; people have been put to death for less wickedness.

Perhaps we have all had meals of that quality. The anxious cook asked, "Did the company say anything about the cooking?"

"No," answered the maid, "but I noticed they prayed before they ate it."

The cooks in the days of Hosea were not equipped with our modern kitchen conveniences, and if the cakes were not to be spoiled, they had to be carefully watched and turned at the proper moment. One can scarcely imagine a more unpalatable article of food than a cake burned black on one side while the other side is uncooked. This is the picture used by Jehovah to describe a portion of His ancient people and might be equally applied to some today.

Having broken away from Jerusalem and the temple worship, the people gradually imbibed the idolatry of their heathen neighbors. While retaining the elaborate externals of Jehovah worship, they shut Him out of their hearts. In all literature there is nothing more pathetic than Jehovah's appeal to Ephraim. They were half-baked cakes.

Like a heartbroken mother appealing to her wayward son, we hear Him exclaim, "How can I give thee up, Ephraim? How shall I deliver thee, Israel?"

Let me point out to you some of the unturned cakes that are too often found within the bounds of all our congregations. They are half-baked.

The Half-baked Have Orthodoxy Without Life

There is in all our churches a considerable company of men and women who are loud in their defense of an orthodox creed. They cherish it as tenderly as a mother fondles her firstborn. They can scent a heresy more quickly than a hound can scent a hare, and woe to the preacher who utters a sentence that seems to conflict with their creed.

They love the doctrine of the divine Fatherhood, and yet they refuse to render Him the obedience of children. They declare that every word of the Bible is inspired but refuse to practice its precepts. Their orthodoxy is on ice. It is like galvanized steel. It is not attractive and appealing.

I appeal to those of you who have orthodoxy in your heads. Let it flow down to the heart. One orthodox act is worth a thousand orthodox professions. Practically all the wrangling that has disgraced the church during the last half of the century has been over theological theories.

One may be as straight as a gun barrel theologically and as empty as a gun barrel spiritually. So often it turns out that fundamental and orthodox Christians become so severe in condemning false doctrine, gnashing their teeth at every sniff of heresy, that they end up without love. One may do a right thing in a wrong way.

The Half-baked Have Piety Without Principle

It is a proof of the deceptive power of Satan that one can often find unctuous piety and commercial crookedness dwelling in the same life. There is the Balaam who desires both the blessing of Jehovah and the wages of unrighteous. His voice is the voice of Jacob, but his hands are the hands of Esau.

There is a continual temptation to have one standard by which we pray and another by which we practice. When one sells principle for popularity, he is morally bankrupt. Piety without principle may look as beautiful as a soap bubble, but it is also as empty. Piety and principle united are like the diamond that wears the sunlight in its heart.

We seem to have confused piety and poverty. We have made them synonymous. The Christian image is at an all-time low.

A woman once said to me, "We don't have preachers like we used to." I responded that I was sure we didn't. She said with concern, "My old pastor never had a suit that would fit and had to ride a horse everywhere he went."

I went to my office to try to figure it out. I could not figure why wearing a suit that wouldn't fit and riding a horse made you such a good preacher. If it would help, I would get an old suit and ride a horse, but I doubt if it would make me a better preacher.

As a preacher, I have to be careful about wise investments and good judgment lest I lose my image as a poor, humble preacher. God wants me to be successful more than I do. I'm not poor; I am rich!

It is not necessary that I inform everyone of my spiritual temperature. Those around me already know.

Revivalist Sam Jones used to tell of a steamboat on the Mississippi that carried such a tremendous whistle that after it was blown, the captain had to anchor in order to get up steam again. He said that the first time it blew, people rushed out of their houses expecting to see an ocean liner and discovered something not much larger than a catboat. The only big thing about it was the noise.

We have done a fair share of boasting during recent years; let us now turn the cake and see if we cannot do some things that are really worthwhile. Let us shut off the whistle and turn on the paddles.

The Half-baked Have Morality Without Religion

These people who have morality without religion are clean cut in their business affairs, and their word is as good as their bond. Your own business is as safe in their hands as your gold would be in the government mint. They fail, however, to recognize the trinity of human virtues: "To do justly, love mercy, and walk humbly with God."

The first two are conspicuous in their lives, but the third is absent. Toward their fellowmen they are honest and kind, rendering them all that is due, while toward God they are both unkind and unjust, withholding both the faith and the service He asks. On the human side they have thoroughly cooked the cake, while the divine side is neglected.

One may be honest toward his neighbor and forget God, but he cannot be honest toward God and forget his neighbor.

Let us not lay on God's altar the mere scraps and leftovers of our time and our ability, but the very best that we have in our treasury.

"Nothing that is morally wrong," said Gladstone, "can be politically right."

Theodore Roosevelt was right when he said, "To educate a man in mind and not in morals is to educate a menace to society."

George Fox, the famous Quaker, was a great practitioner of the discipline of quiet waiting upon God. He counseled his followers to relinquish their agitated and intense frame of mind and gradually rise up through silence into the very thought of the Highest; until, as Longfellow has said, "God alone speaks in us."

The Half-baked Have Zeal Without Knowledge

Of those who have zeal without knowledge their enthusiasm for God and their zeal for the cause of Christ, cannot be doubted. In defense of their creed they are prepared to face the martyr's death or are ready to send to the stake those who oppose the truth as they understand it.

They are like the disciples who wanted to call down fire from heaven upon the Samaritans who did not gladly receive their Master.

Zeal must be guided by the torch of truth. The most unchristian things in the world have been wrought in the name of Christianity. Zeal without knowledge is unpalatable.

The wife said to her hubby, "The two best things I cook are meat loaf and apple dumplings."

He sheepishly replied, "Well, which is this?"

By all means let us have zeal, but let it be according to knowledge.

A minister from out of town had been invited to preach at the local Episcopal church, and the rector was courteously attending him.

"Do you wish to wear a surplice?" he inquired.

"Surplice!" exclaimed the visiting clergyman. "I'm a Baptist. What do I know about surplices? All I know about is a deficit."

The preacher met a young theologian leaving his Sunday-school class. "Johnny, who broke down the walls of Jericho?"

The little boy straightened up and with a belligerent voice said, "I don't know who done it, but I certainly didn't."

The preacher went into the Sunday-school room and approached the boy's teacher. "I just saw Johnny Smith out in the hall, and I asked him who broke down the Jericho wall. He told me that he didn't do it."

The teacher looked at the minister and said, "Well, if Johnny said he didn't do it, then you can depend upon it. He is very truthful."

The preacher thought this was odd. He relayed it to a deacon. The preacher told what the boy had said and the teacher's response.

The deacon said, "Now, preacher, the Smith family are good contributors. Why don't I pay for the damage, and we'll forget the whole thing."

Boy's Essay on Anatomy

Your head is kind of round and hard and your brains are in it and your hair is on it. Your face is the front of your head where you eat and make faces. Your neck is what keeps your head out of your collar. Your neck is hard to keep clean.

Your shoulders are sort of shelves where you hook your suspenders. Your stummick is something that if you do not eat often enough, it hurts and spinage don't help it none.

Your spine is a long bone in your back that keeps you from folding up. Your back is always behind you no matter how quick you turn around.

Your arms you got to pitch with and so you can reach the butter. Your fingers stick out of your hand so you can throw a curve and add up rithmatic.

Your legs is what if you have not got two you cannot get to first base. Your feet are what you run on. Your toes are always what get stubbed.

And that's all there is of you except what's inside and I never saw it.

AUTHOR UNKNOWN

The Half-baked Have Enthusiasm Without Faithfulness

These people who have enthusiasm without faithfulness are adept at launching new schemes, but scarcely have they begun to build by one plan when they want to pull it down and adopt another.

Enthusiasm without faithfulness is like a ship without a helm.

A minister went on a lecture tour and was met by the press in every city for an interview. To one group of reporters he told what his lecture was about and recited much of the lecture. When he had finished, he begged the reporters, "Please do not publish the material I have just recited to you, because once the public knows what I'm going to talk about, they will lose interest in attending my lecture." The reporters promised to keep it off the record.

But one overenthusiastic reporter headed his article: "Minister tells stories that cannot be printed." The reporter was zealous in honoring the preacher's request but not according to knowledge.

A preacher in south Texas had this experience at a revival. He was preaching on the security of the believer when a woman began to shout, "Praise God!" She kept it up. She refused to stop. She had to quit, or the preacher must quit. He asked her kindly once or twice to permit him to go on, and she got worse.

Finally, he called a deacon and asked him if he could do anything to quiet her, and he said, "Yes."

"Well, do it," said the preacher. The deacon stepped over and whispered in her ear, and she stopped dead still. After the service, the preacher said, "Deacon, what did you say to her that stopped her so suddenly?"

The deacon replied, "I just asked her for five dollars for foreign missions."

The Half-baked Have Desire Without Decision

Those who have desire without decision feel an interest in religious matters and, in their hearts, devoutly wish they had enrolled themselves as followers of the Galilean.

If you have wished it in the past, will it now, and join

the ever-growing host which is soon to take up the great shout, "Alleluiah, for the Lord God omnipotent reigneth!"

In *My Conversion*, Leo Tolstoy wrote, "Five years ago faith came to me: I believed in Jesus Christ, and all my life suddenly changed. I ceased to desire that which previously I had desired, and on the other hand, I took to desiring what I had never desired before. That which formerly used to appear good in my eyes appeared evil and that which used to appear evil appeared good." Before his conversion, Tolstoy had acquired fame and fortune through his great writings. But he was unsatisfied.

"I fought duels," he wrote. "I gambled, I wasted my substance wrung from the sweat of peasants and deceived men. Lying, robbery, adultery of all kinds, drunkenness was my life." His conversion, one of the most dramatic of modern times, gave his life a new purpose and meaning and, he affirmed, an abiding satisfaction.

Don't Quit

When things go wrong, as they sometimes will,
When the road you're trudging seems all uphill,
When the funds are low and the debts are high
And you want to smile, but you have to sigh,
When care is pressing you down a bit,
Rest if you must, but never quit.

Life is queer with its twists and turns,
As everyone of us sometimes learns,
And many a failure turns about
When he might have won had he stuck it out.
Don't give up, though the pace seems slow—
You may succeed with another blow.

Often the goal is nearer than
It seems to a faint, faltering man—
Often the struggler has given up
When he might have captured the victor's cup.
And he learned too late, when the night slipped
 down
How close he was to the golden crown.

Success is failure turned inside out—
The silver tint of the cloud of doubt.
And you can never tell how close you are;
It may be nearer when it seems afar;
So stick to the fight when you're hardest hit—
It's when things seem worst that you mustn't quit.

ANONYMOUS

Many times our desire is not our duty. We wrestle in finding the will of God. I found this little poem among my father's papers. George Macdonald expresses the inclinations that each of us has had at one time or another.

What Christ Said

I said, "Let me walk in the fields;"
 He said, "Nay, walk in the town;"
I said, "There are no flowers there;"
 He said, "No flowers, but a crown."

I said, "But the sky is black;
 There is nothing but noise and din";
And He wept as He sent me back—
 "There is more," He said, "there is sin."

I said, "But the air is thick,
    And fogs are veiling the sun";
He answered, "Yet hearts are sick,
    And souls in the dark undone."

I said, "I shall miss the light,
    And friends will miss me, they say";
He answered me, "Choose to-night
    If I am to miss you or they."

I pleaded for time to be given;
    He said, "Is it hard to decide?
It will not seem hard in heaven
    To have followed the steps of your Guide."

I cast one look at the field,
    Then I set my face to the town;
He said, "My child, do you yield?
    Will you leave the flowers for the crown?"

Then into His hand went mine.
    And into my heart came He.
And I walk in a light divine
    The path I had feared to see.

As Jehovah spoke of Ephraim, so He may speak to us.
Are we cakes not turned? Are we half-baked?
  Orthodoxy without life;
    Piety without principle;
      Morality without religion;
       Zeal without knowledge;
        Enthusiasm without faithfulness;
         Desire without decision.

Beware, lest we are cakes not turned.

5

Take Along a Bit of Honey

And their father Israel said unto them, If it must be so now, do this; take of the best fruits in the land in your vessels, and carry down the man a present, a little balm, and a little honey, spices, and myrrh, nuts, and almonds.

Genesis 43:11

There was a severe famine in Canaan. The pale horse of hunger was galloping through the streets. The cold finger of death and misery was pointing at every home. The cries of hunger chilled the heart.

Some time before, grain had been purchased in Egypt. Because of the long continuance of the famine and the complete consumption of the grain, it was necessary to make another trip to Egypt.

The old father, as the head of the family, understanding full well the grim future, called his sons before him to discuss the matter. Father Israel, along with his sons, knew that this was the only way. The sons, knowing this, realized that it was their duty to explain to the old father

81

that they could not see the Prime Minister of Egypt without their youngest brother, Benjamin, accompanying them. The thought of young Benjamin going with them was almost too much for their father, Israel, to bear. Skillfully the eloquent Judah reasoned with his aged sire. Since it was inevitable that Benjamin must go, Jacob made some suggestions.

He said, "If it must be so now, do this; take along the best fruits in the land in your vessels . . .

a present,
  a little balm,
    spices,
      myrrh,
        nuts,
          almonds,
            and a little bit of honey."

Life is a serious business. Before we realize it, we are burdened with heavy responsibilities. There are discouragements, failures, and heartaches peppered with a few joys. We look back over the rugged path to realize that this is life. This matter of living is one of the required courses in life and cannot be left out. We must travel the rocky roads of monotony. Many fail right here. We must cross the sharp stones of personality. There are the hot deserts of defeat along with the marshes of obstacles. Along with John Bunyan's Christian, we must pass through the Slough of Despond. There are too many like Pliable who turn and return to the old life. Some fail to escape the quicksands of flattery. The road of life is ahead.

Yet, we must live noble, lofty, full, buoyant Christian lives. The Bible clearly points out the way. It is Christ's way.

The advice of father Israel has echoed down through the corridors of time. A few wise hearts have grasped it. Listen to it again. "If you must go, take some choice fruits, balm, myrrh, and almonds and a little bit of honey." So, as you travel the road of life, don't forget to carry along a little bit of honey.

When the Tension Is High, Carry Along a Little Bit of Honey

We are living in a world marked by tension. Many responsible men believe that it has reached the breaking point. I know that it is true in the business world. My hat is off to the modern businessman. When I get to feeling sorry for myself, I go look up a businessman and ask him about business. That's all it takes. I believe this is one of my greatest discoveries. It is true that other people besides preachers have problems. When the tension gets high, better carry along a little bit of honey.

The tension gets high in school life sometimes. This reminds me of the story of a young, ambitious schoolteacher who was anxious to get off to a good start. She asked one of her older students, "Have you read Shakespeare?" She waited for his answer.

"Yes," he replied, "that is, if he hasn't written anything recently." Better take along a little bit of honey.

Tension gets high sometimes in home life. There is the story of a man who said he never saw an unhappy marriage. As a matter of fact, all marriages are happy, he said. It's the living together that's rough.

When I was inaugurated as president of Dallas Baptist College, Dr. Willis Tate, chancellor of Southern Methodist University, made this profound statement: "Doctor Thorn, I do not know what the trustees are paying you, but I can assure you that it is not enough." Little did I realize the profound truth of that statement.

Tension gets high in the church sometimes. To a young preacher his early churches always stand out in his memory. Several years ago I had been called to a little country church. It was one of the greatest thrills in all of my Christian life. One Sunday we were to observe the Lord's Supper. The week before I read everything I could find on the Lord's Supper.

Upon my arrival that Sunday morning, they informed me that all the arrangements had been taken care of. At the service, to my amazement, there was only one big glass and everyone drank from this same container. The old deacon had a great bushy moustache, and as he would drink from the common cup, his moustache seemed to float on top. It looked to me like they could have had a moustache cup. Now this worried me no end. Something had to be done.

Finally the answer came to me. There was only one thing to do. It was the only logical thing to do. So the next time we observed the Lord's Supper, I drank first, and then passed it on to my faithful deacon. It didn't bother me so much after that. It is so necessary to carry along a little bit of honey.

Life in general gets mighty rocky. During this time one comes to realize the value of a little honey. In the Lincoln-Douglas debates, it appears that Douglas, by all standards should have won the debates. But Mr. Lincoln had that little extra ability to get hold of people. On many occasions he completely disarmed Mr. Douglas with a little country story. He knew how to use a little bit of honey just at the right time.

In Dr. James Whitcomb Brougher's marvelous little book *Life and Laughter,* he gives this wonderful little story from the life of Abraham Lincoln:

> On one occasion a committee of Republican senators met Mr. Lincoln and urged him to make a clean sweep of his cabinet. They wanted him to appoint six other new members in addition to Mr. Stanton. The tall man listened with patient courtesy to the request; then with a twinkle in his eye, he said, "Gentlemen, your request for a change of the whole cabinet because I made one change reminds me of the farmer who had much trouble with skunks. They annoyed his household at night, and his wife insisted that he get rid of them. One moonlit night he loaded his old shotgun and stationed himself in the yard to wait for the intruders. After some time, his wife in the house heard the shotgun go off. When the farmer presently returned, she asked him, 'How did it go?'
>
> "He replied, 'I hid myself behind the woodpile and before long there appeared seven skunks. I took aim and blazed away but only killed one. He raised such a fearful stink that I concluded that it was best to let the other six go.' "
>
> The senators left, laughing heartily, and noth-

ing more was said about the reconstruction of the
cabinet.

With the spirit of forgiveness and good will, combined
with a sense of humor, you will not find many occasions
to lose your temper and give into an emotional explosion
that will give you wrinkles and gray hairs.

When Responsibility Is Heavy, Carry Along a Little Bit of Honey

One does not live long until he begins to feel the pressure of economics. Along comes a family with all its responsibilities. A man immediately buys insurance
policies so that his children will have the opportunities
in life. He struggles with the premiums for twenty years.
It is difficult, but it will be worth it. Application papers
have just arrived from college, but alas, his son has just
eloped with the neighbor's girl.

Not long ago a young man called and wanted a confer-
ence to discuss an important matter. As he walked into
the office, I could tell that he had a problem. After a few
moments of discussing the weather, I asked him what his
difficulty was.

"Sir," he said, "I have a financial problem." With this
he pulled out a few bills and laid them on the table. He
said, "There is just no way to get them paid."

Realizing that something had to be done, I began to
search my mind for suitable words. For some unknown
reason I opened my desk drawer and pulled out a large
stack of envelopes and said, "These are the bills I
couldn't pay." He looked at me with great surprise. A

smile came over his face. He caught the message.

"Well," he said, "things are not as bad as I thought." He went away happy.

Men do strange things under the pressure of economics. Not long ago an amusing thing happened. There came a knock at my office door. To my response a young man walked in. He had that sheepish grin on his face. I knew immediately that he wanted to talk to me about matrimony. When they look like this young man, there is not very much that you can do. Have you ever noticed that most of them want to know about matrimony after they are in it?

After a few moments I asked him if he had what was necessary, two dollars. Then I asked him if there was a girl who would marry him. As I looked at him, there was a question in my mind.

"She is in the car," he said.

After he brought her in, and we visited together, I performed the ceremony. He then pulled out a roll of bills. "Preacher," he said triumphantly, "How much do I owe you?"

I used to say, "Whatever you think she is worth." Of course, that never paid off. Then he started laying the bills down on my desk. He slowly counted them out, "One, two, three." When they get past two, I get mighty happy. "Four, five, six," he slowly counted. When they get past five, I get worried about them. After he reached seven, he slowly turned and looked at his new bride and then picked up two of the dollars and put them back in his pocket.

It has been my custom lately to receive the fee in my hand, and when they turn to see what they have done, I tighten my fist. Oh, it pays to carry a little honey.

The responsibility of a job or great undertaking weighs heavy on a man. In church work there rests a tremendous burden and responsibility on the pastor. My father, who was a faithful preacher of the Word, gave me some good advice when I was beginning my ministry.

"Bill," he said, "when you get out on the field and you don't know what to do next, and as a matter of fact, you don't know what's going on, let me give you some advice." He then looked at me and said, "Just stand in the corner and smile and keep your mouth shut." I have been in the ministry about thirty years now, and I have spent about twenty-five years of it in the corner smiling. Listen, it works! When responsibility is heavy, you had better carry a little bit of honey.

When People Misunderstand You, Carry Along a Little Bit of Honey

You will not have to live long until people will misunderstand you. They will misinterpret your finest intentions. They will rearrange your motives. They will add to everything you say. If you could hear what they say you said, you would not recognize it. I wonder if we have lost the art of listening.

Dr. J. D. Grey would make calls to church members before the working day began. Early one winter morning he dialed a number he thought to be that of one of the men of the church. An unfamiliar sleepy voice answered. J. D. inquired, "Is this 555-8849?" The strange voice coldly retorted, "No! This is 555-8840." Quick as a dial tone, Grey said, "Friend, you have just picked up the wrong telephone."

Better carry a little honey.

Not long ago I was invited to speak to a local Parent-Teachers Association meeting. After jotting down my assigned subject, I went to great length to get all the materials possible on the subject. When the day arrived for the meeting, I was well prepared to give my part. The president introduced me and said, "Doctor Thorn will come now and speak on the subject for the month, 'The Beauty of Truth.' "

My heart sank within me. Struggling to the platform, I delivered my speech, "The Beauty of Ruth." I realized again the value of a little bit of honey.

This little story was related to me some time ago. Let me tell it in the first person so that you can get the effect that I did.

Preparation was being made for a big church wedding. It was to be a major production. The bride's mother had everything under control. I could sense that she was doubtful as to my ability to do the job. She had the latest word on everything connected with weddings. I found out later that she herself had eloped and been married by a justice of the peace.

Nevertheless, the wedding was started as scheduled. The couple was standing before the altar. The hour was most solemn. After the introduction, I turned to the groom and asked him to clasp right hands. He thought I said, "Clap hands," so in the middle of the ceremony this lad began to clap hands. Hurriedly I turned to the bride and said the same. She then began to clap. So I just joined in and clapped with them. In a few moments we were able to continue the ceremony. People will misunderstand you. Better carry along a little bit of honey.

My good friend Dr. John Haggai tells a story which well illustrates this point. A man sped up to a drugstore and asked the druggist if he had anything for the hiccups. The druggist, without a word, hit the man between the eyes and knocked him down. The man slowly got up and asked again, "Sir, do you have anything for the hiccups?"

The druggist replied, "You don't have them anymore, do you?"

The man replied, "No, I never did, but my wife out in the car does."

On one occasion an elementary teacher was anxious to teach her young pupils the evils of alcohol. It was her noble desire to impress their sensitive minds with a strong object lesson. She set before the class a small cup of alcohol which she promptly labeled. Then she put a worm into the cup of alcohol, and it soon died. She asked the class if they could see the lesson taught here. Johnny raised his hand. He then related, "This teaches that if you have worms, drink whiskey." You know, some people just think that way.

Paul was misunderstood when he wrote to the church at Thessalonica. He urged them to be ready for the return of the Lord. They thought that Paul meant that the Lord was coming immediately. The old Apostle had to write them a second letter explaining the first letter and telling them to get back to work.

So when men misinterpret your actions and misunderstand you, remember the words of Jacob, "Carry along a little bit of honey."

When You Become an Important Person, Carry Along a Little Bit of Honey

It has been my privilege to know many great men. These men were from all fields of endeavor—medicine, politics, education, religion, and so on. From this experience I can make this observation: You never have to worry about a big man in a big place. It is small men who somehow get into big places that give you all the trouble.

Confucius said, "What the superior man seeks is in himself, but what the small man seeks is in others."

Some people know a lot more when you try to tell them something than when you ask them something.

Dr. J. B. Cranfill, in his excellent volume *From Memory,* tells about Russell H. Conwell, the long-time Baptist preacher of Philadelphia. Mr. Conwell gave his famous lecture "Acres of Diamonds" more than five thousand times. One of those times was in Dallas, Texas. The text was about a diamond hunter who went to South Africa prospecting for the precious stones. He bought ten acres of land and built his little shack. He sought for years to find diamonds. His seeking was fruitless. Finally, worn-out with his long and fruitless quest, he died. His neighbors decided to bury him on his own land. When they dug his grave, they found that his entire ten acres was underlaid with diamonds.

Dr. Cranfill said that he would never forget the other story that Dr. Conwell told on that occasion. It was the story of a Boston bully, who, half-drunk, said to a bystander, "You stand here while I go into that saloon. There are twelve men in there, and I expect to go in and pitch them out headfirst, one by one. As I throw 'em out, you count 'em." The bystander agreed and soon heard a deafening uproar in the saloon, followed by the appearance, headfirst, of a bruised and battered man.

The bystander, true to his promise, cried out, "One." Whereupon, the man said, "Stop the count; it's me."

There are too many people who believe every compliment given to them. This has been the downfall of many a preacher.

Several years ago, while I was serving a wonderful country church, a kind, motherly woman gave me a compliment. Following the service, she took me by the hand and said, "You are a model preacher." Naturally, in those days, compliments did not come often, so I wanted to make the most of it. On the way home I told my wife about it. She did not say much. I guess she knew better. During the next few days I called it to her attention several times. She apparently was not as impressed as I was.

Finally, she took about all she could. After a moment she had found the word *model* in the dictionary. She looked at me and read: "*Model,* a small imitation of the real thing." That's all it took for me. Later a lady said that I was a "warm" preacher. I figured that one out for myself. It meant "not so hot."

If there was ever a time when you need to take a little bit of honey, it's when you begin to feel your importance.

When You Plan Your Life, Carry Along a Little Bit of Honey

Laughter is the surplus of life. It is the bubbling over of the emotions. It is a kind of spasm of exuberance—a delight that makes the thorax cackle. You may laugh your way into the hearts of people; you can seldom cry your way in. If you weep, people will feel sorry for you, but they will soon tire of it when you continue to parade your troubles before them. Laugh and they will love you. Smile for exercise; it will strengthen the muscles of good humor. A few years ago I heard a man close a wonderful speech with this well-known line: "Laugh and the world laughs with you; weep and you weep alone." We should weep alone. Remember, weeping is often a selfish, childish performance.

Life is a serious business. I do not mean to go through life laughing all the time. This would be foolish and a waste of life. Life can be saturated with the joys that refresh and keep our outlook clear.

Leroy "Satchel" Paige of baseball fame records for us his philosophy of life:

Avoid fried meats which angry up the blood.
If your stomach disputes you, lie down and pacify
    it with cool thoughts.
Keep the juices flowing by jingling around gently
    as you move.

Go very light on the vices, such as carrying on in
society. The social ramble ain't restful.
Avoid running at all times.
Don't look back. Something might be gaining on
you.

Dr. Charles Haddon Spurgeon, the mighty preacher of
London, used many funny stories in illustrating his lec-
tures to his students. Dwight L. Moody, the evangelist,
always enjoyed a good story at the end of a hard day's
labor.

Recently I heard of a man who had great difficulty with
cursing. It was a major problem to him. Being greatly
concerned about it, he decided to go to see his minister
for help. After discussing the problem at length with the
preacher he was still not satisfied. Being a practical man,
he wanted something tangible in the solution. The wise
pastor, seeing this, suggested that every time he felt like
cursing, he should sing a hymn. This was satisfactory,
only the man didn't know many hymns. The preacher
gave him a hymnbook and then sent him on his way.
After a few days, the man returned to see the pastor. His
face was beaming.

"How are you doing?" asked the pastor.

"Fine," was the reply. "Pastor, I am making progress,
but I am ready for a new hymnbook."

A sense of humor is an absolute necessity.

Try to develop humor as a personal trait. It will keep
you from an overestimation of your own importance, will
keep you from worry, and will prolong your life. When

the door squeaks, you had better add a little oil. So in this great undertaking of living, remember the advice of father Israel:

"If you must go, remember to take along some choice
   fruits,
      balm,
         spices,
            myrrh,
               nuts,
                  almonds,
                     and don't forget to carry along,
                      A little bit of honey."

6

The Fountain of Youth

. . . thy youth is renewed like the eagle's.
                                        Psalms 103:5

Ponce de Leon, the Spanish conqueror and explorer, engaged in an effort to locate the fabled "fountain of perpetual youth." He had heard from the Indians of an island named Bimini which contained a marvelous fountain in the waters of which old age could be thrown off and youth renewed. In search of this, he set out in March, 1513. Ponce de Leon grew old trying to find the fountain of youth. How true today. We grow old trying to stay young.

Recently I read a most interesting book written by Renee Taylor about a small nation called Hunza. Hunza is tucked away in the mountains of West Pakistan. It is accessible only by trail. The people live to be 120 years old. There is little illness, and eighty-year-old women retain beauty of youth. In 330 B.C. a division of Alexander the Great's forces broke away, took Persian wives, and lost themselves in the vastness of the Himalayas. Those returning from expeditions to Hunza claim it to be the land of the "fountain of youth."

There is something in being young that makes it one of the most desirable things in the world. You cannot pay the average old-timer a higher compliment than to say to him, "Why, you're as young as ever!" And likely enough, he will cut an awkward caper to prove your words true.

"That pain in your leg is caused by old age," the doctor told his elderly patient.

"That can't be," said the man. "The other leg is the same age, and it doesn't hurt a bit."

Golda Meir on her seventieth birthday said, "It is not a disgrace to be seventy, but it is also no joke."

A woman begins to notice she is no longer young ten years before she has any real need to worry about it; a man begins to notice he is no longer young ten years after everyone else has tacitly accepted it.

Why should we ever lose the freshness of youth, the sense of wonder and romance of life? The possibility of retaining what the Bible calls "the dew of thy youth," is delightfully manifest today. Time was when men and women used to dress according to their years. Now mother and daughter exchange garments along with grandmother.

Not long ago I visited a very fine restaurant. While looking over the menu I noticed a little poem which I copied:

Methuselah

Methuselah ate what he found on his plate
And never, as people do now,
Did he note the amount of the calorie count;
He ate it because it was chow.
He wasn't disturbed as at dinner he sat,
Devouring a root or a pie,
To think it was lacking in granular fat
Or a couple of vitamins shy.
He cheerfully chewed each species of food,
Unmindful of troubles or fears
Lest his health might be hurt
By some fancy dessert,
And lived over nine hundred years.

Most people are afraid of getting old. To them age is like "love and smallpox—neither can be hid." Women are sensitive about their age. An old lady, living next door to the preacher, became ill. To show his friendly interest, he told his young son to run over and "find out how old Mrs. Johnson is." The boy went and came back quickly, saying, "Mrs. Johnson says it is none of your business how old she is."

Cornelius Vanderbilt at eighty added more than $100 million to his fortune. Wordsworth earned the laureateship at seventy-three. Adolphe Thiers at seventy-three established the French Republic and became its first president. Verdi wrote *Falstaff* at eighty. Stradivari made his first violin after he was sixty. Tennyson at eighty-three wrote "Crossing the Bar." Daniel DeFoe was seventy when he wrote *Robinson Crusoe*.

There are some very practical suggestions I would make.

To Discover the Fountain of Youth, We Must Keep the Heart Young

Youth is not a matter of clothes or cosmetics. Youth is retained, not by keeping face and form young, but by keeping the heart young. Hearts may grow old in the twenties or leap with the exuberance of youth in the eighties. When a tired body and a negative mind meet, there is despondency.

Hear Gladstone delivering his speech in the British Parliament at eighty-one and declaring, that if he had died at seventy, the better half of his life's work would have been left undone. See Justice Oliver Wendell Holmes as buoyant of spirit, as keen of intellect, and as full of humor in his nineties as in his youth. Look at Thomas Edison busily seeking out new inventions right up to his death at eighty-five.

Physiologists tell us that in all mammals, except man, the period of life is five times the period of growth. A dog gets its full growth in two years and lives ten; a horse in five years and lives twenty-five. On this basis man should live from 100 to 150 years.

But William James, an eminent psychologist, said that most men are "old fogies" at twenty-five. It is true that most men at twenty-five are satisfied with their jobs. They have accumulated a little stock of prejudices that they call "principles" and close their minds to new ideas. They have ceased to grow. When a man ceases to grow, no matter what the years, then and there he begins to be old.

Emerson said, "Nothing great was ever achieved without enthusiasm."

Some people seem to be emotionally dead.

Dr. J. D. Sandefer, long-time president of Hardin-Simmons University, used to tell this little story to the students' delight.

A man and his wife went to the county fair. A pilot was there taking people for a plane ride for five dollars per person. The couple wanted to go, but they thought the price was too high.

"Take us both for five dollars," he said. The pilot wouldn't cut the price, but the man kept arguing.

"Tell you what," the pilot said at last. "You pay me ten dollars. If neither of you say a word, I'll give you your money back. It won't cost you a cent."

The couple agreed and got into the plane. The pilot did all the stunts he knew but did not hear a sound. When he landed, he turned and said, "You didn't say a word, did you?"

"Nope," the man shook his head. "But I almost did when my wife fell out."

There is no failure in life like the failure to keep young. We cannot prevent time from rolling on or this earthly tabernacle from getting out of repair. But this is no reason why the spirit that inhabits it should dry up and shrivel.

To Discover the Fountain of Youth, We Must Keep the Life Clean

A young heart is a clean heart. Nothing ages body and soul like sin. The Satan of the Bible is old—old and cynical—and to be cynical is to be old.

And, of course, sin, and especially the sin of impurity, robs the heart of the capacity for love, robs the mind of resilience, robs the soul of aspiration, and hurries off into old age. As Robert Burns said, "It hardens all within and petrifies the feeling."

It would be valuable to remember the words of Talleyrand, "Behold, eighty-three years have passed without any practical result save fatigue of mind, great discouragement for the future, and great disgust for the past."

Listen to this, written by Byron at thirty-seven;

> My days are in the yellow leaf;
>   The flowers and fruits of love are gone;
> The worm, the canker, and the grief
>   Are mine alone.

An old, old man at thirty-seven.

Being good and doing good are the most romantic, adventurous, and exciting occupations in the world. Let no evil habit come upon you to steal away your youth. Time puts its inevitable mark upon us, but sin ages before the time. It puts premature wrinkles in the brow, furrows on the cheeks, weariness in the eyes, a stoop in the shoulders, a burden on the heart, and a blight on the brain. It digs graves for the burial of faith and hope and love and youth.

The toastmaster discovered as he was about to call on a clergyman to say grace, that the clergyman had not arrived. He looked over the guests and noticed an actor who could ad lib fluently. In desperation he called on the actor.

The actor calmly arose, bowed his head, waited for silence and then said in his most resonant and impressive tones, "There being no clergyman present, let us thank God."

Let us pray, "Create in me a clean heart, O God; and renew a right spirit within me." With these possessions, your youth will be renewed like the eagle's.

To Discover the Fountain of Youth, We Must Keep the Enthusiasm of Youth

If the heart is to be kept young, one must preserve the enthusiasm of the young. If ever you find yourself getting critical, censorious, and pessimistic, it is not a sign that you are getting wise; it is a sign you are getting old.

There are some, however, in whom the candles of enthusiasm seem to burn brighter as the years go by. Enthusiasm is the greatest asset in the world. It overwhelms and engulfs all obstacles. It is nothing more or less than faith in action.

Educator William Lyon Phelps declared in his autobiography, "I live every day as if this were the first day I had ever seen and the last day I should ever know." No wonder that he died a young man at seventy-eight.

Laughter is the sunshine of the soul; the happiness of the heart, the privilege of purity and the echo of innocence.

It destroys depression, dispels dejection, mangles melancholia, and banishes the blues.

It is the ripple of the river of delight, the sheen of the silvery smile, and the glint of the gold of gladness.

Without it humor would be dumb, wit would wither, smiles would shrivel, and dimples would disappear from the cheeks of the world.

We must learn the value of spiritual enthusiasm. It is summed up by the Honorable Dan Liu, who served as chief of police of Honolulu and was voted the most popular man in the Hawaiian Islands. The chief said simply, "Due to Christ I never buckled under any anxiety and have always been sustained in the dangers of my profession." Spiritual enthusiasm cancels worry.

It is enthusiasm that wins ball games. It is enthusiasm that puts pep in pepper. It puts magnet in magnetism. It puts the person in personality. It is enthusiasm that makes a leader and makes a life victorious. Put all the enthusiasm you can into your work, and you are sure to win.

To Discover the Fountain of Youth, We Must Have the Forward Look

Nature knew what she was doing when she put our eyes, not in the back of the head but, in the front. She meant that we were made to look forward rather than backward. It is a characteristic of old people that they live in the days that are gone, forever harking back to the good old days.

Julia Ward Howe, the famous novelist, was asked by a friend if she minded growing old. "No," was her reply, "because the sugar is at the bottom of the cup." Remember, life is measured not so much by its longevity but by its intensity.

If you want to be young when you are old, then you must act a little older while you are young.

But, for many, all the good things of life are behind them. They wish they were children again. These people are old. They are sitting on the sidelines watching the rest of the world go by. They are like a jingle that I once read:

> The lightning bug is brilliant,
> But he hasn't any mind.
> He blunders through existence
> With his taillight on behind.

Dr. Henry Porter, in his unique little book *Toward the Sunrising,* tells of the life of Dr. Walter Brooks. Dr. Brooks was the noted black preacher of the Nineteenth Street Baptist Church in Washington, D.C., for more than sixty years. He was a native of Richmond, Virginia, where the first fourteen years of his life were spent in slavery. He began his ministry as a Presbyterian, but the young woman he married was a Baptist. He was soon an active member of his wife's church. Dr. E. H. Pruden, former pastor of the First Baptist Church of Washington, D.C., tells us that when Dr. Brooks had been pastor of the church for thirty years, he got down on his knees and told the Lord that he was sixty years old and that he was going to resign and make way for a younger man. Dr. Brooks said that the Lord asked him, "What is wrong with My making a younger man out of you?" So he stayed on, with renewed youth, for thirty more years.

When he resigned, he was past ninety. He was still vigorous and still looking forward.

Grow old along with me!
The best is yet to be,
The last of life, for which the first was made.
                              ROBERT BROWNING

Nothing is sadder than not to know the truth of Browning's words; nothing is more rewarding than living by them. There is as much of the "last of life" to live as the first, maybe more. So, accept the blessed idea that the best is yet to be, and you will live a rich, full span on this earth, wasting none of it in future fears or vain regrets. But, of course, the last of life is to be a serene and wonderful time beyond all other.

To Discover the Fountain of Youth, We Must Look Up and Live

The master secret of perpetual youth is religion. I do not recall the source of the quotation, but I agree that "any religion that does not help to keep young people young has something deeply the matter with it." As the Prophet Isaiah declares, "Even the youths shall faint and be weary, and the young men shall utterly fall: But they that wait upon the Lord shall renew their strength; they shall mount up with wings as eagles; they shall run, and not be weary; and they shall walk, and not faint" (Isaiah 40:30, 31).

Don't grow old. It is unpardonable folly. Look up to the ageless God. One of the grandest promises of the

Bible is found in the Book of Ruth: "And he shall be unto thee a restorer of thy life, and a nourisher of thine old age . . ." (Ruth 4:15).

We want to cry out with David: "Cast me not off in the time of old age; forsake me not when my strength faileth" (Psalms 71:9).

We ought to pray, "Lord, help me to live until I die."

An Ode to Aging

Careful aging makes good meat
A vintage wine a gourmet treat
A seasoned cheese is recognized
As the one most highly prized;
Old chairs, despite groans and squeaks
Bring fancy prices as antiques
In view of this, I just don't see
Why age does not improve on me!

Age has a way of making us pessimistic.

Two elderly women were talking, and one said, "I am entertaining two locust preachers in my home."

The other laughed. "That was a funny slip; you meant local, of course, dear."

"No, I said locust, and I mean locust."

"But, locusts—why, locusts are things that come in swarms and eat everything in sight and . . . ."

"Don't I know it," snapped her friend, "and I'm entertaining two of 'em in my home this week."

While reading in Deuteronomy, I came across this eye-opener: "And Moses was an hundred and twenty years old when he died: his eye was not dim, nor his natural forces abated" (Deuteronomy 34:7). The amazing thing about this statement is not that he was 120 years old but that "his eye was not dim, nor his natural forces abated." Moses discovered the secret of perpetual youth.

Remember, God has promised to take care of us.

The father of President Woodrow Wilson was a Presbyterian preacher. One day a man observed the Reverend Mr. Wilson riding in a shiny buggy drawn by a sleek well-groomed horse. Noting that the preacher was shabbily dressed, the man remarked, "Mr. Wilson, your horse looks better cared for than you do."

To this remark Brother Wilson replied, "Yes, that is right. For you see, I take care of my horse, and my church takes care of me."

The God of the Bible is young, buoyant, enthusiastic—a God of creative energy, rolling stars over the sky, flinging worlds from His fingertips. He is a God who dreams of saving the world, who sends His angels to sing the joyous songs over the starlit hills of Bethlehem. And when we come to the last book of the Bible, we hear a voice from the throne saying, ". . . Behold, I make all things new . . ." (Revelation 21:5).

To find the fountain of youth,
    We must keep the heart young,
        We must keep the life clean,
            We must keep the enthusiasm of youth,
            We must keep the forward look.

7

Snakebites

And when Paul had gathered a bundle of sticks, and laid them on the fire, there came a viper out of the heat, and fastened on his hand.

Acts 28:3

As far as I am concerned, snakes are taboo. I have absolutely no affinity for these slimy little creatures. The study of herpetology did not come into my degree plan. As a matter of fact, it didn't come into my vocabulary until last week. It has been brought to my attention that there are nearly three thousand known species of snakes. Snakes do not have movable eyelids. They can look at you all day without blinking an eye. Some snakes grow very large. There are stories of snakes that have reached the length of fifty feet. These snakes live far too long for me. One anaconda survived for twenty-nine years in captivity. Snakes often eat other snakes. This shows you what they are really like. All snakes are carnivorous.

They will give up good food to get their fangs into a man. A large python is known to have survived without feeding for four years. They tell me that there are many snakes that will not hurt you. Maybe they won't hurt you, but they will make you hurt yourself!

After a brief reading of the Bible, I knew we were going to have difficulty with these snakes. Even a snakebite kit looks vicious.

The Apostle Paul was on his way to Rome to appeal his case to Caesar. This was his right as a Roman citizen. Paul had been turned over to the emperor's men and was on his voyage to Rome. A vicious storm fell upon the little ship, and it appeared that it would be crushed in the teeth of the storm. The sea was angry and was seeking vengeance for some unknown wrong.

Under the providence of God, the little party escaped to the Isle of Malta. The driving rain and the gusty winds made it uncomfortable. The natives of the island showed them much kindness. They set out to build a great fire for warmth.

Paul was no slacker and was always anxious to carry his load. He refused to be a freeloader. He thought that every man should hoe his own row. He threw himself into the task of building the fire. As he carried a bundle of sticks and laid them on the fire, a viper came out and fastened on his hand. Paul then held his hand over the fire. As the flames seared his hand, the serpent fell into the fire. All eyes were upon Paul, for it appeared that death had at last caught up with him. They waited for him to die. Paul always did the unexpected. He did not die and was able to continue his journey to Rome.

Today, there are still many snakes with which to contend. Many of us have been bitten by these vipers. The poison is seen in our lives.

We May Be Bitten by the Serpent of an Unlovely Disposition

We meet these victims every day. It was well known throughout the little farming community that Farmer Brown and his wife led a cat-and-dog life. Finally, he built himself a cabin in a field behind the barn, moved in and left his wife in the house. One day a neighbor visited him, noticed how immaculate the cabin was kept, and saw on the table a blueberry pie and a pan of freshly baked biscuits.

"Sarah comes in now and then and cleans up a bit and brings hot biscuits and such," he explained. "You know, no man could live with that woman, but she makes an awfully good neighbor!"

Indeed, some are bitten by the serpent of an unlovely disposition. The first symptom of this poison shows up in one's attitude. Attitude speaks louder than words. A poor attitude will lead to difficulty in all areas of life and somehow blinds one to this tragedy. It closes more doors than ability can open. This is usually tied up with plain old selfishness.

Too many of us are like Narcissus. Narcissus was a character in Greek mythology, the son of Cephissus, the river god. Narcissus was a handsome lad and was indifferent to the beauty of others. He was very vain about his own beauty.

Echo, a nymph who was a favorite of the gods, was so wounded by the rejection of her love by Narcissus that she faded away until only her beautiful voice remained. The gods, angered by Narcissus's coldness and Echo's death, caused him to fall hopelessly in love with his own image mirrored in a spring, until he too died and was changed by the gods into the flower that bears his name. There are too many who have actually fallen in love with themselves.

Indeed, it is true: "An high look, and a proud heart, and the plowing of the wicked, is sin" (Proverbs 21:4).

For some reason this unlovely disposition comes out within the family circle.

Dr. I. E. Gates, former president of Wayland Baptist College, tells the little story of a blackmailer. A man received a letter from him which said, "If you do not place five thousand dollars in a hollow stump (naming the location of the stump) by six o'clock tomorrow afternoon, I am going to kidnap your wife."

To this letter the man replied, "Dear Mr. Kidnapper: I haven't the five thousand dollars to do as you requested, but your proposition interests me."

If there is any place that we need kindness, it is in the family circle. Dr. Carlyle Marney, in his book *Dangerous Fathers, Problem Mothers, and Terrible Teens* has an excellent chapter on fathers. He mentioned that he knew of no books on the parental care of fathers. Fathers are no longer a biological incidental; the father has become an economic necessity.

It was a wise mother of whom the story is told that when cross or fretful voices were heard among the children, whether outdoors or in the house, she would call them, "Sing it, sing it." Often the song began, "You cheated, you cheated," or "I hate you, I hate you." But so quickly it changed to smiles and laughter that it became a family proverb, "Never say what you cannot sing."

This unlovely disposition is too many times manifested in our church life.

Dr. Gates also refers back to the days when there was no Women's Missionary Union, when many of the old-timers were against women's having much to do with church affairs. One of these old-time preachers was moderator of the association, and he objected to women speaking in mixed assemblies. One day one of these heady women rose to speak, and the old moderator said, "Sister, Paul forbade women to speak in public, and I must ask you to sit down."

Another woman in the rear of the building, with a high-keyed voice shouted out, "Where would you men be now if it were not for us women?"

The old moderator replied in a stern voice, "We would all be in the Garden of Eden, sister."

Beware, lest you be bitten by the serpent of an unlovely disposition.

We May Be Bitten by the Serpent of Selfishness

This serpent disfigures greatly. It can change the beautiful into the ugly and the sweet into the bitter. It can change the whole personality. Watch the man after he has been bitten.

Every time this man thinks his case is peculiar. His problems are the biggest. His enemies are the most unscrupulous. His jokes are the funniest. His own prayers get special attention. His own virtues are most exemplary. His own faults ought to be overlooked.

A fellow went to a very high-priced psychiatrist and said, "Doc, I've got a problem."

"What's your problem?" asked the doctor.

"Well, I'm married; I've got a car; we have three children; we have a home in the country and a home in the city."

"You don't seem so bad off," replied the doctor. "What's your problem?"

The patient cried out, "I only make forty-five dollars a week."

A big, burly man called at the parsonage and, when the door was opened, he asked to speak to the pastor's wife, a woman well known for her charitable impulses.

"Madam," he addressed her in a broken voice, "I wish to draw your attention to the terrible plight of a poor family in this district. The father is dead. The mother is too ill to work, and the nine children are starving. They are about to be turned out into the cold, cold streets, unless someone pays their arrears in rent which amounts to fifty dollars."

"How terrible!" exclaimed the lady. "May I ask who you are?"

The sympathetic visitor applied his handkerchief to his eyes as he said, "I'm the landlord."

Oh, what selfishness will do to a person!

It is also manifested in ingratitude. This old story always illustrates the point. I have used it so many times.

A mountaineer couple's one desire was that their only son have an opportunity to go to college. To make it possible, they plowed the neighbor's corn, washed the overalls of neighbors, and used the coffee grounds over and over again. The day came when Sam enrolled as a freshman. Time passed and sacrifice became more intense. Sam seldom wrote back home after his sophomore year. Then came the day of graduation. The old man, in his clean blue overalls, was driving up the campus road in an old buggy. Noticing three smart-looking lads, one of whom looked like Sam, he called out to them, "Do you know my boy, Sam? He is graduating."

Sam, looking at his roommates, then at the old man and the out-of-date buggy, turned to them, saying, "Who is that old man? Let's get going." The old man turned the mule around and drove off slowly to his mountain home.

Can life be that cruel? Indeed, it can, for at this very hour there are millions who have turned their backs on God, their Father, and disowned Him to His face.

Many have been bitten by this serpent.

We May Be Bitten by the Serpent of Laziness

This snake is found nearly everywhere and has been very active. Its poison has been spreading for a long time.

A man was told one morning that he looked tired. "I am tired," he said. "Last night I was reading in a magazine that a man turns over every fifteen minutes. I weigh two hundred pounds, so last night I moved six thousand, four hundred pounds and just one thought of it makes me tired."

An old mountaineer and his son were sitting in front of the fire smoking their pipes, crossing and uncrossing their legs. After a long period of silence, the father said,

"Son, step outside and see if it's raining."

Without looking up, the son answered, "Aw, Pop, why don't we just call in the dog and see if he's wet?"

It actually takes a lot of energy to live. If we are not careful, we will use it all up living. A man may be allotted threescore and ten years. If he is, he will spend twenty-three years and four months of it asleep. He will work nineteen years and eight months. He will spend ten years and two months in religion and recreation. He will spend six years and ten months eating and drinking. Six years will be spent in traveling. Four years are spent in illness. In this time he will spend two years dressing. After thinking this through, no wonder we are tired.

A gentleman had trained a large dog to pull a light garden plow. Whenever anyone came about, the dog would set up a terrific barking, as if he would tear the intruder to pieces. The gentleman, who had observed the ways of the dog carefully, explained that there was no danger in the dog, that he only barked so as to have an excuse for not plowing. Our churches seem to be filled with these barkers. As a matter of fact, there are just about as many in the pulpits.

When theologian, Dr. John Broadus said the "workers never grumble and the grumblers never work," it was close to the exact truth. Working and grumbling do not harmonize. They are two opposite forces. Religious work promotes soul health, as physical work promotes bodily health. The most ear-splitting calamity howlers are the men who have quit honest toil and taken to crying hard times, blaming it all on somebody else.

The poison this little serpent of laziness spreads!

Too many of us are lazy physically. Every individual who is seeking to get through life without toil needs to have read to him the little motto which hangs in many business houses:

> Don't let the bacilli of Shirk
> Get into your system and lurk;
> If from friendship or pity
> You're put on a committee,
> Don't be a dead one—you work.

The man of wisdom is so right. "Go to the ant, thou sluggard; consider her ways, and be wise: Which having no guide, overseer, or ruler, Provideth her meat in the summer, and gathereth her food in the harvest. How long wilt thou sleep, O sluggard? . . ." (Proverbs 6:6–9).

An elderly man got a job in a war plant during the war. He had to work very hard. There was never a minute to rest or get his breath. As soon as he finished one assignment, there was someone there to give him another. They almost worked him to death.

After a few days, he went to the main office. "Do you have a Bill Simpson working here?" he moaned.

"You say 'Simpson?' " the man replied. "Let me see, yes, we have a Bill Simpson working here."

The old man asked, "Do you spell that S-I-M-P-S-O-N?"

The man nodded in the affirmative.

As the old man turned to walk away, he was heard to say, "Thought you might have that down as S-A-M-S-O-N."

There is little danger that we will work ourselves to death.

We are lazy mentally. The reason for this, I believe, is that we do not use our time wisely. The *Houston Chronicle*, a few years ago, called attention to a news story out of Los Angeles which showed the relationship between car ownership by high-school pupils and their grades.

A school principal found in a study he made that not a single straight A student he questioned owned an automobile, but no less than 83 percent of the pupils who failed in their studies did.

He found that only 15 percent of the B students owned cars, but 41 percent of the C students and 71 percent of the D students owned cars. The principal believes the result of this survey is typical nationally.

As to that, it would be difficult to prove, but apparently the *Chronicle* is justified in its conclusion that "high-school joy riding and good grades don't mix."

It is not the cars in themselves; it is the time they consume. Indeed, the trouble is that of being lazy mentally.

We are lazy spiritually, also. Have you ever had the spiritual grippe? Some of the symptoms are: a sort of indisposition to do anything, weakness in the knees, loss of backbone, raspiness or harshness of voice, and a peculiar "all gone" or tired-out feeling which occurs especially in meetings. It may include being rather peevish and fretful at times, disinclined to pray, ill at ease during hot sermons. There is also lethargy or creeping paralysis, which gradually steals over the being, together with tightness in the pocketbook, unpleasant sensations in the chest, and alarming symptoms about the heart, frequent "spells" of sputtering and complaining, coughing up excuses, dimness in the eyes, and dullness in the ears. In short, a general rundown condition, accompanied by terrible chills of fear and trembling, hot flashes when things go wrong, and awful attacks of doubt and uncertainty.

If you are suffering from an attack of this character, whether it be acute or chronic, send at once for the Great Physician (a little delay may prove fatal). This spiritual grippe, or as it may be more technically termed, "American back slidicus," is a most deadly disease. It has been traced to spiritual laziness.

I know of so many in our churches who are doing so much, yet would do more if they were asked. Then I thought of the following lines I read somewhere: "God never goes to the lazy or to the idle when He needs men for His service. When He has work to be done, He goes to those who are already at work." When God wants a great servant, He calls a busy man. Scripture attests to this fact.

Moses was busy with his flock at Horeb. Gideon was busy threshing wheat in the winepress. Saul was busy searching for his father's lost sheep. David was busy caring for his father's sheep. Elisha was busy plowing with twelve yoke of oxen. Nehemiah was busy bearing the king's wine cup. James and John were busy mending their nets. Matthew was busy collecting customs. Saul was busy persecuting the friends of Jesus. Are you busy enough for God to use?

We May Be Bitten by the Serpent of Inconsistent Living

"Ye are our epistle written in our hearts, known and read of all men" (2 Corinthians 3:2).

One of Emerson's terse and telling epigrams is this: "What we are sometimes speaks so loud people can't hear what we say."

It is said that Adelina Patti, one of the most famous of all opera singers, once lost her passport and sang a song to prove her identity. Her voice and her name were in harmony.

We are reminded of Ulysses. While he was absent at the siege of Troy, his faithful wife, Penelope, was annoyed by suitors. After waiting ten years and thinking Ulysses dead, she at last gave the promise of her hand in marriage to the one who should shoot an arrow through twelve rings with the bow Ulysses had used in other days.

In the meantime, Ulysses arrived. Disguised as a beggar, he was present on the day of the trial. The first thing to be done was to bend the bow in order to attach the string. One by one the suitors stepped forth to prove their prowess and, amidst the laughter and jeers of their companions, confessed it was a task beyond their strength to perform. Then spoke Ulysses, "Beggar as I am, I was once a soldier and there is still some strength in these old limbs of mine. Let me try."

The suitors hooted at him and demanded that he be turned out of the hall for his insolence. But to gratify the old man, Penelope bade him try. Then, lo, with ease, he bent the bow, adjusted the cord to its notch, and sped the arrow unerring through the rings. It was Ulysses, indeed, and Penelope threw herself into his arms.

What little use it is to profess, if our actions belie the profession we make. It is not so much for us to say that we are Christians, as it is to prove it by the life we live.

Indeed, this old serpent has inflicted many with the poison of inconsistent living.

It was seventeenth-century writer Ralph Venning who said, "In religion not to do as thou sayest is to unsay thy religion in thy deeds, and to undo thyself by doing."

Cowardice asks, "Is it safe?"
Experience asks, "Is it polite?"
Vanity asks, "Is it popular?"
But conscience asks, "Is it right?"

Beware of the serpent of an unlovely disposition.
Beware of the serpent of selfishness.
Beware of the serpent of laziness.
Beware of the serpent of inconsistent living.